Graham Bradshaw is a former journalist who worked at the *Leicester Mercury* and the *Eastern Daily Press* in Norfolk as well as the *Mansfield Chronicle Advertiser*. He returned to the East Midlands and now lives in Mansfield with his wife.

To all those who helped to bring about
a happy ending to my tale.

Graham Bradshaw

PAGES IN A LIFE

A Reporter Remembers

AUSTIN MACAULEY PUBLISHERS™

LONDON • CAMBRIDGE • NEW YORK • SHARJAH

A CIP catalogue record for this title is available from the British Library.

ISBN 9781528905800 (Paperback)
ISBN 9781528907064 (ePub e-book)

www.austinmacauley.com

First Published 2022
Austin Macauley Publishers Ltd
1 Canada Square
Canary Wharf
London
E14 5AA

Contents

Foreword and Forearmed 9

1 Black Panthers and Blue Noses 11

2 In Your Own Words 16

3 Cast of Characters 24

4 Court in Time 35

5 Inky Noses and Computers 42

6 Transports and Delights 49

7 Death and Destitution 58

8 Foreign Fields and Twin Towns 70

9 Seats of Learning and Perishing Politicians 82

10 A Last Word 94

Afterword: Pages from the Past 95

Foreword and Forearmed

THE AIM OF this book is to entertain. It reflects events that happened to me and around me when, in a non-PC age, I reported for a local newspaper. It is not intended to be a well-researched social history but just my memories. Some of my experiences were great and some were a pain in the bum. Many happened on football grounds and in court where the expression, 'Eeh, that's vexing!' was seldom heard, so if bad language upsets you then perhaps you should not read on. Or feel free to supply your own asterisks/hieroglyphics. The aim is to entertain and not offend. Thank you.

1 Black Panthers and Blue Noses

ROGER, THE PHOTOGRAPHER, bounced up and down a couple of times while I did an elegant dance, like somebody trying to put out a fag end with each foot. Come to think of it, I wished one of the three of us was a smoker; maybe all of us could have huddled round a glowing coffin nail for warmth. Not for the first time Steve, the other photographer, remarked that the night air was bracing in the extreme although, being a poetic soul, he may have quoted the immortal line, we thought, from *Steptoe & Son*: "I'm colder than the icicle on a penguin's chuff."

And, not the first time, I thought that the fact that I was standing in a freezing courtyard behind Mansfield police station in the middle of a winter night instead of being tucked up in a warm bed was my own damned fault.

I had been finishing off some stuff in the office about teatime when Steve came in. "Are you going to the press conference?" he asked.

"What press conference?"

He raised his eyes to heaven. "Only the bloody Black Panther bloody press conference."

Rumours and details of the story had been emerging all day. Two local coppers in a Panda car had been held at gunpoint before arresting a man who had been hunted throughout the country. Never mind all this fair trial malarkey, Steve was sure it was the notorious Black Panther, as suspected.

I had been working on the *Mansfield Chronicle Advertiser* – or *CHAD* as it was known in the town – for several

11

years but one of my colleagues had spent many more years reporting for the *Nottingham Evening Post* before joining us. He had been out keeping up on developments.

"Where's Albert gone?" asked Steve. Another good question to which I had no answer. "There's going to be a press conference about 8.30 at the cop shop: surely we've got to have somebody there." I could only agree.

Plan A had been that I would end the working week by meeting a couple of friends, Paul and Martin, for a beer. I rang them and said that I was considering passing on the social invitation. Both said that working on a local weekly paper it was by far the biggest story I would be likely to be involved with, even if peripherally, and I wouldn't forgive myself for missing out. The Black Panther had committed about seven post office robberies, killing anyone who got in his way, before he kidnapped and killed the teenager Lesley Whittle. It would be good experience, they said, which rather worried me. It was an continuing trend that whenever a job was 'good experience' it seemed to involve me being bored out of my brain, half-drowned, frozen to death or a combination of them all. I told them an outline of the details that we had so far and it only tended to confirm my view that I should join our photographers at the press conference.

It was to prove a somewhat cagey affair because what was said had to conform to the rule that someone was innocent until proved guilty in a court of law. However, the officers who had led the hunt for the Panther had travelled to Mansfield and all the indications were good that a massive hunt had finally yielded results.

The local policemen involved in the capture were Stuart McKenzie and also Tony White, the latter of whom I knew at least by sight. He once flagged down my car as I was starting to drive home in the late evening. I wound down the window and he said, "It's OK, it's just that I knew it was your car and I wanted to make sure it was you driving it and not a car thief." It struck me as good policing as well as being very courteous to me. I was very grateful for being stopped like that and gave him my thanks, which was better than having a shotgun stuck up his nose. Whatever else was in doubt about that night, what was sure is that those two local coppers were heroes and made our streets safer for everyone.

The two officers were perhaps lucky to escape at least serious injury as the Panther's gun went off when Tony saw his chance and pushed away the shotgun, which had been jammed in his colleague's armpit as the Panda was travelling through Rainworth. The two found allies in two men from the queue for the local chippy. Together they got the Panther handcuffed to railings.

Local legend is that one of the have-a-go heroes suggested that the coppers might like to take the opportunity, while they waited for back-up, to get revenge on the man who had subjected them to a terrifying ordeal. When he was told they could not do that he is alleged to have said, "Well, I friggin' can." Certainly, when a picture the Panther could be published later, his face showed some wear and tear. Probably it was inflicted during the struggle, but if not nobody in the crowd at the scene that night would have worried too much.

Later, after the trial verdict, I had moved on to sub-editing and we laid out a spread about the Panther. One of the illustrations was a cartoon from a copper who was obviously something of an artist too – showing a panda upper-cutting a panther.

The plan was to take the suspect – shortly to be confirmed as Donald Neilson – to Kidsgrove, where Lesley Whittle had been kidnapped. So a phalanx of journalists filed out into the station yard and the wait began.

The yard out the back was ringed with garages and the gaggle of journos took what shelter they could find. We were under cover at least, but there were no doors, and setting a cop car on fire for the warmth did not seem to be a good idea. So we settled down and waited... and waited... and... well, you get the idea.

Finally we got some relief as a police van swept into the yard. Two coppers got out and threw open the back doors. The flash of camera bulbs lit up the entire yard like a mix of Christmas decorations and the Blackpool Illuminations. In the centre of this pool of light was the figure of a Mansfield pisshead. He stood blinded and bemused and then an enormous grin spread across his face and he spread his arms wide. He continued to grin as the coppers helped him to wobble into the station to go and sleep it off, along with waving like the Pope bestowing benedictions. He was followed by an enthusiastic round of applause.

If his wife or partner needed any proof of where he was that night there were hundreds of pieces of photographic evidence available.

Then we all stopped chuckling and went back to waiting. As I did so I mused about the future. Even if this bloke was not the Panther, he was definitely a bad 'un. We later learned that apart from the shotgun he had a whole load of knives and equipment for doing no good. There would eventually be a trial and the hope was that he would be behind bars for life. I, of course, am not a vindictive man but I dearly hoped his cell would be cold.

Eventually the back door to the police station opened. This was promising. There had been no reason, apart from boredom, why we had previously got so excited about a vehicle coming *into* the station yard since it was hardly likely to be involved with the main business. This time a whole crowd of policemen emerged and formed up into the tunnel, several deep. They were certainly taking no chances. Then they joined us in another wait.

I ended up standing behind a young copper who proved friendly and chatty and had obviously been involved with the suspect. "I'll say one thing for the bastard," he said.

"He'd certainly kept himself in shape. He has the body of a much younger man." He looked down wistfully at his own physique. I'm sure he could handle himself when the need arose, but I would call his stature portly rather than athletic. Being more along the lines of an under-nourished whippet myself, I sympathised.

We have all viewed scenes of crime suspects emerging from or being put into police vehicles with the cliché of a blanket over their head, but this one felt very different. Probably it was just that I was close to the action this time. The fact that it was dead of night and the flashbulbs were made so blinding that added to the drama. Whatever, after so much time crawling by, it seemed to be quickly finished – the clump of car doors, the roar of an engine and the brief flare of a vehicle's lights and then a strange quiet followed.

Steve and Roger got their gear together. Our conflab on events was over pretty quickly as well. They would have film to develop, I would have notes to sort into order and we would all have tales to tell.

At the time I was scrounging off my parents in Nottingham. I thought about going back into the office, but not for long. It was an advantage to be working on a weekly newspaper. I jumped in my car, turned the heater up full blast and headed for home.

2 In Your Own Words

"ARE YOU AN extrovert or an introvert?" the editor had asked during my interview for the role of junior reporter.

"Pervert" was the true answer, according to another reporter when she later heard of the conversation. The problem with that was that I never did detect any trace of a sense of humour in the bloke who was deciding my fate.

I remember that as I said introvert I was convinced that the truth would cost me dear. To my surprise and relief he said that was good. "Any idiot can wander about with a notebook asking questions but it's what happens in front of a typewriter that matters."

Well, this particular idiot begs to differ. It was going out and meeting people and finding the right questions to ask and the right approach that I sometimes had trouble with.

The job I came to hate the most was attending the annual dinner of various clubs and organisations. I was OK on reporting the speeches but first I had to sit through a meal I didn't particularly want among people who, while generally very welcoming, I had never met.

Certainly my interviewing career had its ups and downs.

The passage of time dims memories. I don't really remember all the details of an interview I conducted with a tall, imposing and distinguished man but I bitterly remember the feeling.

He explained slowly and carefully to me about how he had solved something by harnessing all the best qualities of a 'grangejabbitoscillator' and asked if I followed him. I assured him, airily, that I had three at home and asked my next question. He gave me a look that would have melted a bar of chocolate on a table three miles away.

"You said you understood. You obviously have not understood a word that I've said."

I don't remember my reply but I seem to think that when I exited the scene I did so by walking *under* rather than through the door. Not a good experience but a valuable lesson in getting things clear in my mind if I was about to write about them.

Being situated near the heart of Sherwood Forest, we frequently had visitors from all over, which presented interview opportunities. I did *not* conduct one when a film crew were busy near the Major Oak. The young woman presenter was bouncing around and gabbling away, looking stunning in a short, mock-Robin Hood outfit over very tight tights. I decided my Japanese was too rusty to gaze into her eyes and ask for her impressions of our area. Sorry to be old fashioned and non-PC, but I, like every other straight fella around, settled for watching her with lust.

Another non-triumph was Dave Allen, the Irish comedian. He must have been touring, probably staying in Nottingham or Sheffield. Again the visit was on a time schedule but I should have tried to grab a quick chat. I could have started with the honest opinion that some of his TV sketches were brilliant. My impression that he was a good bloke, without arrogance, was enforced when he finished his fag and kneeled on the forest floor to make a small hole and bury the nub end.

Mind you, he did harbour a grudge that I hadn't spoken to him. Years later when I was in Norfolk and he was on TV he deliberately timed the punchline on a sketch when he knew I was just taking a swig of wine. I damned near choked to death.

I was also left a bit out of breath by a phone conversation with a friendly and down-to-earth clergyman who was involved in a dispute with his local council. I asked him if he would be registering a serious complaint, which seemed justified. He said he would let it go because he wanted the council's assistance with a project he had in mind. "Let's put it this way," he said. "If you want somebody to do something for you, you don't kick him in the balls first." Thank you, vicar.

One interview was neither good nor bad, just different. Mansfield does not have a long maritime history, probably because the sea is miles away. It was, therefore, worth a story when a bloke decided to build a sea-going craft in the back yard of a terraced house in the suburbs. It would need a long slipway to launch it. I rang his front door bell. He only opened the door a fraction and peered at me. I explained why I was there.

"I suppose you'd better come in then," he said, "but don't take too long." I entered the house and followed him up the stairs. He then removed his towel and got back into his bath before the water went cold.

I got a bit of a dubious look from his wife when she returned with the shopping and found me interviewing her naked husband while leaning on the bathroom wall.

The newspaper got a story and a good picture later of the boat being craned above the roofs of neighbouring houses.

There were a couple of interviews that I remember fondly but only with hindsight. One was with Brass.

Times change. These days you can visit places like Matlock Bath any old day and find a mob of motorcyclists. When they remove their helmets they are seen to be middle-aged and respectable men and women with a shared interest.

At that time the Hell's Angels had a *bad* reputation. It wasn't helped by a Marlon Brando film and all the battles between Mods and Rockers that had engulfed seaside resorts.

The police obviously felt the same way. They told us that they were expecting trouble at nearby Kirkby-in-Ashfield. The Angels had booked a hall for a 'chapter meeting' or get-together but a council committee chairman had taken a late decision to cancel the booking. The thought was that Angels who had travelled a long way would be a trifle vexed about that.

This was another fine mess that a photographer got me into. Both Roger and myself had been busy in the morning. I had a 'night' job – evening strictly – but the afternoon was quieter. Roger thought we ought to have a run out in his little CHAD van to see what was happening in Kirkby.

We found a scrawled note on the hall door saying that the event was off in Kirkby but that he Angels had gone off to a pub in Shirebrook, so that's where we headed. If you don't know Shirebrook, especially then, think pretty houses in tree-lined streets. Then forget it. It was a pit village that had a reputation for being somewhat rough round the edges.

We found the pub with no trouble, but I'm not sure we were pleased about it. There was a wall round the place as we approached and to me it seemed there were hundreds of leather-lined man mountains perched on them, all with pint pots in their hands. I began to change my mind about being constipated.

We could hardly pretend to be new recruits for them, rolling up in a van with *Chronicle Advertiser* plastered all over it. "Let's look round the back," said Rog.

He parked by the side of the road where we could see

a large car park leading to the back entrance of the pub. There were only a few Angels in sight so it looked more promising. We took the time to stop and stare, but then I thought there was no point in putting it off.

I had got halfway across the road when I heard a voice calling out behind me. "Hang on, Graham," said Rog, "I can't let you die on your own." I feel that right there was the start of a friendship of 40-plus years and counting.

We approached a couple of the blokes who seemed to be posted as guards near the entrance. They did not smile in welcome. I told them who we were and why we were there, but it wasn't easy. For once it was not a cold day but my teeth still seemed to be chattering for some reason. One bloke turned to another and grunted, "Fetch Brass."

I had nearly said, "Take me to your leader," like in all the worst alien jokes.

When their leader appeared he had quite a bit of facial hair, like most of them, but he was not that big by their standards. He did, however, have an air of authority and did not seem to be a wise choice to make for anyone looking for a fight.

While I felt it was a good interview I did not quote him verbatim very much. I did a bit of editing myself and left out the multiple references to fornicating and people, like the council bloke, who were born out of wedlock.

However, Brass did have reasonable points to make. He pointed out that the Angels could not get together like this regularly. They were not looking to cause trouble but felt let down. If the local council had concerns about their behaviour they could have checked with them or, at least, have cancelled the booking much earlier in the week so the Angels would have had time to make other travel arrangements.

At one point a somewhat older bloke came up and told us that he had been an Angel for many years and we should ignore the reputation. He was attending the event with his son, who was following in his tyre tracks.

As the interview went on I did not worry so much. This was not so bad. Then Rog said he wanted to get some photographs.

"Right," said Brass, "Come through the pub. You'll be OK – provided you stay close to me." I started to worry again.

Brass took us to a large yard with a wall round, the place we had seen when we first approached. He shouted orders and a goodly number of statuesque Angels gathered behind him.

While Rob took his pictures I stood with my notebook and reviewed my scribblings. I then became puzzled. The sky was blue but rain seemed to be falling in my bit of the yard. I looked round and, for the first time, got a smile from some of the characters on the wall. They had been playing a game of pulling bits of brick out of the wall and trying to land them on my notebook, without bouncing them off the top of my head first. I smiled back at them. It seemed the sensible thing to do.

We did stick close to Brass. But this little group was joined by a tall, rangy bloke who was even scruffier than the rest. He was full of smiles but they did not inspire confidence. He latched on to Rog and began asking lots of technical questions about his camera. He said more than once that he would like to have a camera like that. The trouble with photographers is that they love their cameras. If any of this lot had wanted my notebook, they could have had it and a dozen Biro pens in an instant. Rog would not have parted with his camera.

Brass, as we had realised, was no fool. He had seen the situation and, quite quietly, told this bloke to adjourn to another part of the pub. Then Brass, the gentleman, thanked us for coming to see them and invited us to have a drink with him. The pub was heaving with hairy, hard-drinking motorcyclists and all I wanted to do was to get back to our little van. Instead, Rog and myself realised how thirsty we were. We must have been, because it took us no time at all to down a drink and get the hell out of there.

The day after these events I found a photograph on my desk. It showed a grim-looking Brass in the foreground with a mob of other Angels in the background. Visible in the far background was another figure. A pen circle was around its head, with a caption bearing the legend: 'Mad Dog Bradshaw'.

I came away from the meeting with the Hell's Angels with a couple of things. One was some more 'good experience'. Another was my own private force-field.

Let's just say that some of the Angels had a different concept of personal hygiene than the majority of us. My evening job that day was a review of a concert by the Cantamus, a local choir with an excellent reputation (and still going strong). I thought they were fully up to standard that evening. I enjoyed both the music and the space to stretch out. As I remember, nobody else would come within three rows of me in the theatre.

Both myself and Rog got the same benefit from our encounter. If anyone gave us any hassle we could invite them to mend their ways. Otherwise we'd send our friends Brass and the Boys round for a word!

Times *do* change. These days you are as likely to see a woman as a bloke reporting on football, but not then. Certainly the women I worked with later would not have thanked any news editor for sending them to a football match.

I must admit I had rather fallen out of love with football. My Dad took me to Meadow Lane to watch Notts County when I was a youngster and I played in occasional matches while at the *CHAD*. So I tended to go off on a

Saturday morning to Field Mill to cover Mansfield A team fixtures.

This particular morning the crowd was seven men and a dog – and the dog was asleep. Three of us from different papers were in attendance but we had a privileged position. We had the comfort of seats indoors overlooking the practice pitch which was staging a match which did not get up to cup-final standards. The teenagers involved were frankly the only ones that were enthusiastic. My mind wandered.

Then all three of us realised that the referee was pointing and the Stags' left back, a lad called Billy Grozier, was trudging off the pitch with his head down. We had a quick debate and none of us had seen anything which explained why Billy had got his marching orders. I was happy to volunteer to break the boredom by investigating.

I found Billy, who looked about 14, sitting in the home dressing room all alone. His head was in his hands, his socks were down and his boots were against the far wall where he had thrown them.

"Hello Billy," I said like a long-lost uncle. "Why did you get sent off?"

The poor wee lad looked up at me with pain showing in his eyes.

"Don't fucking ask me. Me and this fucking youth went for the fucking ball and the fucking ref said that's fucking it, you're off. I never fucking touched him," he elaborated.

I went back upstairs to my colleagues.

"Why was Billy sent off?" they chorused.

"Mr Grozier was somewhat mystified by the match official's ruling," I told them.

Rumour has it that Billy later gave up his footballing ambitions and became an elocution teacher.

3 Cast of Characters

IF YOU HAVE a few moments, perhaps I could give you a quick guided tour.

The main hub of the Mansfield of today consists of Westgate and the Market Place. In those days you could get from one to the other by means of an alleyway. In that little area, close to the town's cinema, was Linney's shop and the offices of the *CHAD*, which was another part of the Linney empire. The two were linked by a reception which saw a lively flow of people wanting to leave adverts, reports of weddings and obituaries and to lynch reporters. Just down at a bend in the alley was a pub.

I can best describe this hostelry by detailing one lively encounter. The *CHAD* receptionists heard sounds of a kerfuffle and looked out to see two working ladies knocking lumps off each other. They apparently thought they each had the rights of the, er, attentions of a single client. The bloke sized up the situation and made himself scarce, leaving the two to continue grappling.

Reporters could get to the working areas of the newspaper either through the back of reception or, after hours, further down the alley. This area became sealed off with a heavy, portcullis-style wooden gate. This was added after a reporter one night almost inadvertently became part of a threesome, tripping over the thrashing legs of a couple on a trolley on wheels designed for other uses.

At the far end of the alley was a chippie. The smell of fish and chips drifting about could be lovely. However, on some mornings when the deep fat fryers were being cleaned out, the smell was awful.

The staff door led to a smallish entrance area with the door to the compositors' room to the right. Next to that door was the blessed drinks machine.

There was an another interesting feature. You could lift a wooden flap and pull down a metal lever to turn off electricity to the floors above. The reporters, on the first floor, worked irregular hours. If you did not hear the sound of footsteps going down the stairs due to bashing on a typewriter you could suddenly be plunged into darkness. An erudite shout of "Oi!" usually produced an answering call of "Sorry." If not, the person had already gone and you had to come down the stairs in darkness to find the lever.

I have inherited a healthy regard for a cuppa from my mum. I must have walked thousands of miles up and down those rickety stairs with a tray full of drinks. Whatever other journalistic skills I gained, I became bloody good at remembering who had what on the drinks run.

The photographic department was on the floor above and, if I remember correctly, that was crowned with advertising. It was not unusual during the evening to take a phone call from a woman trying to reach her husband who was one of the bosses up there. Rumour had it that he recruited attractive young women and taught them to display more than just adverts.

After you opened the door to editorial you walked down a short corridor and emerged into the reporters' office. On one side of the corridor was the office of the editor and then the sub-editors.

The door to the editor's office was usually open. It

should have been a welcoming sign but it often just revealed him alone, staring into space.

On the other side of the corridor was the office of Stan, the sports editor, next to that of Jeremy, the chief sub.

I never envied Stan particularly. A lot of his time seemed to be spent poring over stuff submitted by people from sports clubs, sifting it and sticking bits of paper together. When it appeared in the paper much of it was in the paper's smallest size of type, 4.75 point. Stan, however, seemed a fairly happy chappie. He used to work in the hosiery trade and much preferred what he was doing now. Stan was one of the people who took a fatherly tone to me and tried to help shape my journalistic outlook.

Jeremy, unlike the editor, knew what he was doing.

One of the things that Jeremy enjoyed was a visit, several times a day, by a girl who looked just out of primary school and who worked as a 'gopher'.

What she meant to say, each 10am, was: "Good morrow. I trust you are well on this bright morning. Have you, perchance, items to be conveyed to the photographic department for processing?" What came out, without fail, was "Eyup, gorowt?"

Later I had quite a few battles with Jeremy, both verbal and physical. We sometimes had play fights and had disputes but I always respected him. Respect is a valuable commodity and has to be earned.

Just inside the reporters' room was a desk occupied by Betty, the editor's secretary. Bet was at the heart of the operation, certainly socially. Much of the chat and humour in the department revolved around her.

On the other side of the office was the desk occupied by Harry, the news editor. He was an expert on local government and was often consulted by folks who wanted to know if and how it worked. His desk was packed with council reports and agendas and it was also the home of the reporters' diary where there was a list of jobs, each bearing the initials of the reporter who was to carry out the task. I caused a small sensation from the start. My initials were the same as those of the editor! People loved the thought of him covering a coffee morning or dog show.

Another feature of the diary was that whenever you consulted it you came away with a liberal dressing of tobacco because Harry was a pipe smoker. Ron, one of the other reporters, used to roll his own fags so there was no escape.

The staff included younger folk in Mick and Tony and Carole, Helen and Roma.

Mick always appeared friendly, calm and laid-back, which I envied. I would also have loved to be as good at shorthand as him but mine was only ever adequate. When there were tricky phone calls to make, Mick was lined up on the other side of the desk, listening in with headphones and making a verbatim note of what was said. What I did pick up from Mick was his casual greeting of "Hello, Shitheap." My mum was appalled when I greeted Roma that way when she rang me at home.

A daily ritual in the reporters' room was Roma putting on her make-up. It was like witnessing one of the great artistic endeavours. Despite my initial doubts, she and I forged quite a close and long friendship.

Thinking about it, my friendships seem to last many years. Maybe my parents should have named me Fido.

A later friendship was with a reporter called Heather. We were unsure of each other initially. The turning point was when Heather drew my name in a 'Secret Santa' where you bought a little Christmas present for a colleague. I received a parcel of chocolate, sweets or similar in Christmas wrapping paper. I also received a plain brown paper bag. I peered inside.

"What's this?" I asked, I thought not unreasonably.

"It's you," said Heather.

"But it's an onion," I pointed out.

"Yes well, you're just like an onion: you have to peel away layers to get to know you." It was not the only experience I was given in learning how others viewed me.

The *CHAD* was an ideal training ground for working in newspaper journalism. These days in local papers you find several pictures of the same event with virtually the same caption on each. We were told to get the names of everyone pictured. It helped build a relationship with a photographer if you took names for him or her. Rog once gave me a picture of the opening of a much-needed zebra crossing. It was OK that I was captured in the background watching local councillors parade ceremonially across it but it was unfortunate that the pen in my hand was sticking up. It looked for all the world like I was waving two fingers at them. Not me, honest ref.

Another photographer when I started was Janice. I made an effort to watch my language in the early days but reality tended to change my good intentions. I was telling Janice that someone had been testing my patience and her suggested answer was, let's say, straight to the point. I went with Janice on a visit to a local colliery. Afterwards we stood together in the miners' welfare having a drink. That day I got some definite 'lucky little git' looks from the blokes having a pint. Boy, was I smug.

There was a thriving coal industry round about Mansfield. Ron, a more experienced reporter, generally covered anything to do with the National Coal Board and the unions. It was pretty serious stuff.

However, there was one union dispute that had a lighter side before the great strike that signalled the end of the industry.

Union members were under pressure about whether to take strike action. One of the wives got her pals together for a campaign to influence the decision. If their blokes decided the wrong way there would be no naughties for them.

The story made the Nationals and gave everyone an excuse to have their say, including a woman we'll call Big Ada, who offered to give free services which were being denied. She then decided she would disappear to a safe house until the furore died down.

One night in the office I picked up three phone calls within 10 minutes, each with a different female voice, telling me: "Big Ada is living at…" and spelling out the exact address.

We covered masses of charity events like bring & buy sales and were expected to get the names of every stallholder. Another old favourite was the golden wedding. I went to see one couple who said, as some did, that they never fell out, except… When pressed they said they had a row early on in married life and it was a beauty. The wife got so annoyed that she lashed out at the dining table. Unfortunately she was holding what was then a common feature, a heavy glass sugar bowl. She ended up feeling guilty and he felt pain as they stitched his head up. After that, they lived happily ever after.

The most important member of staff for me, at least in the short term, was Les. I don't know exactly how long he had been working there before I started but he became my mentor and we went out on jobs together quite often. We got along pretty well, despite me trying to put him in the A & E at hospital.

One dark late afternoon we were wandering around a school trying to find a teacher. I can't remember any more details. The school was not an old and creepy building like the *CHAD* offices but it was largely in darkness and a bit spooky in the quietness. For a laugh as I opened the door to the 17th empty classroom I jumped back in fear. Les was just behind me.

"You daft bugger, I nearly swallowed my lighted fag!" he gasped.

I was later able to take on the mentoring role for a trainee. Having given them the Bradshaw lecture on checking every fact, I took them to a long-service ceremony at the local HQ of the electricity board. The receptionist smiled at me and patiently told me that I wanted the gas board offices just down the road.

There were several occasions when I thought my journalistic career would be the shortest on record.

Another fairly tedious job was taking the names of mourners at funerals – a task now regularly taken on by the undertakers' staff. At my first one I approached a tall bloke and asked his name. He patiently spelled out that his name was Ian Linney – only the boss of the company for which I was working. Les told me not to worry because it was not unreasonable that I didn't know him after such a short time on the paper.

One of the first times I went with Les for funeral names we were approached before the event by a clergyman. He smiled and chatted with us amiably for several minutes before going into the church. Les told me he was Bob Warburton, the Rural Dean.

He must have been another one, like Dave Allen, to harbour a grudge against me for some reason. Many years hence he was to conduct my wedding. He asked the congregation only to use one door of the church, especially when throwing confetti and gold coins at the happy couple. Then he patted me on the shoulder and said: "Graham, it's too late to run for it before the bride arrives because I've locked the back door."

Then there was the time I was told quietly to report to Jeremy's office and I thought I must have done something dreadful. There were two of them waiting for me. Jeremy waved a copy of my efforts with a "What do you call this? Are you trying to get us all hung?" The paper was my claim for working expenses and it was too little. I was given a masterclass on how to fill them out. I was entitled to claim for a meal if I was miles from the office at lunchtime or had a 'night job' in the evening. Other skills I never learned, but I soon became as quick and imaginative as anyone in the office at doing expenses.

Then I went to a fund-raising event for Guide Dogs for the Blind. I relaxed somewhat. Any reason to talk to dogs is fine by me and I met a woman who said she had been a columnist on the *CHAD* previously and had set up a strong link. The paper is still helping to raise enough money to finance guide dog training.

She thanked me for coming to cover the event and I told my new pal airily that you had to keep folks happy. I went back to the office and mentioned to Bet about the former reporter I had encountered, asking what had happened to this Anne character. "She married Mr Greenslade," she told me. Only the big boss on the editorial side and a national figure. Oops.

A very early job was a 'topping out' ceremony. Tree planting I like. At least, no matter who pretends to do the work you end up with a new living feature in the landscape. It's fair enough to mark the completion of a building project with a last inscribed brick on the top; the problem is that it tends to be some bigwig who gets to put a blob of mortar on it. Even worse, it's a politician who gets pictured wearing a hard hat, grinning and pretending that he's done something useful for a change. Ring any bells?

This ceremony was at the new maternity unit at King's Mill Hospital.

For any non-locals still with me, the hospital site was big then and is even bigger now. From the top of the unit you got a view of a main road, surrounded now by a supermarket, fast food outlets and industrial units. But on the other side of the road is King's Mill Reservoir. This is a haven, particularly for water birds, and a comparatively quiet area for people to have a walk and spot wildlife.

It's a big area of water, this was the middle of winter and the crowd of journos, councillors and health officials were perched on high. As these events always do, it took time for everyone to get in place. It felt as if the wind had picked up a battery of razor blades on its journey over the res.

We stampeded downstairs into the warmth for refreshments. Hot drinks would have been great but I think I ended up with a half of bitter. Two photographers had gone along, one news and one commercial, and they decided that a whisky would warm them up. That started to work quite well, so they had a second.

The commercial bloke had a parcel of pictures to deliver somewhere else on the hospital site. I'd swear we went round the same roundabout three times in their little van before he staggered off to the office, booted open the door and chucked the parcel in.

We somehow got back to the office. I'm not sure about the drink and drive laws at the time but I thought there must be some about being drunk on duty. I left the photographers to wobble further up the stairs to their department, went to my desk, opened a drawer and tried to crawl in. I was stone-cold sober but I thought it safer to wait for the booze fumes to dissipate.

There was a young woman called Helen on the reporting staff when I started although she moved on before too long. She did, however, have quite an impact on me before she did so.

I went back to the office quite late one dark night to write up my story. The door to the editorial department had a large weight attached so that it closed gently behind you. Helen was alone at her desk and had not heard the sound of the door before I materialised, spookily, at the entrance to the office. She jumped so high her head nearly hit the roof. I apologised profusely for frightening her and started to type out my story. A couple of minutes later she finished writing her copy, put it in the subs' basket and put on her coat.

"Sorry I was so scared," she said. "But you have been told about the ghost, haven't you?"

"Er, no."

"Well, a young reporter got quite depressed for whatever reason." She pointed to a large hook in the ceiling of the wonky old building. "He hung himself from there. Anyway, I'll probably see you tomorrow. Bye."

The editor needed to have no worries about my abilities in composing stories. I bashed out that particular one bloody quick.

Another character who was not there very long was Mickey. We met one night when I was alone in the office, typing up my 'night job' story. I began to wonder whether the place was indeed haunted. I heard stirring noises, almost like whispering. I looked round fearfully but saw nothing. Then I realised that the noise was close beside me. I looked down and the paper moved in a large cardboard box used as a litter bin to reveal two dark eyes regarding me and a whiskery nose twitching. OK, Mickey was a mouse – what do you want, originality?

Thereafter we kept some lonely evenings at bay, sharing companionship and the remains of the odd sandwich until, sadly, I went and spoiled it one Saturday morning.

This time I was sharing the office solely with Carole. "Oh, look," I said, "Mickey has come to see you."

Carole was quite a lively character but I had never

known she could move that fast until I mentioned the word 'mouse.' We've all seen the cartoons of course, but like lightning Carole was stood on her desk.

"Kill it, kill it," she shrieked, while doing a little dance. Since we had such opulent surroundings, I was able to find part of a house brick lying around. In a scene reminiscent of a silent comedy film I chased Mickey under desks, brandishing the brick. Mickey was my pal and I had no intentions of injuring him but felt I had to stop Carole from having hysterics. Mickey got me out of the predicament by disappearing into a hole at the base of one wall.

Carole could be quite feisty so, no doubt, was in the editor's office first thing on Monday morning threatening to call in pest control unless action was taken. This time Harry came to the rescue. He had a female cat which won the Queen's Award for Industry in producing kittens. In short order Harry had one fewer kitten and the office had a mouser.

My pal Mickey was no fool and, hopefully moved next door. The arrangement did not last for long. Some of us were always happy to make a fuss of the kitten whenever we returned to the office. The editor, being a miserable sod, ordered that the kitten should go the day it crapped in his in-tray. More than one reporter had longed to do the same thing.

4 Court in Time

COURTS, ESPECIALLY, MAGISTRATES' courts were a constant source of entertainment. Talk about 'all human life is here'.

Long before the current fad for a tattoo, the criminal classes in Mansfield had their own club badge on the knuckles. They were a refined lot so I'm sure they wanted the message: "All serving police officers are of very doubtful parentage." However they ran out of digit space and had to settle for ACAB. (Work it out.)

One of my colleagues once covered a Monday morning court after all the fun and games of the weekend. The dock was full of the roughest mob of reprobates she ever saw – except for a well-groomed young man in a smart suit. She asked why he was sat there "with that lot" and was told that he had glassed his brother in the pub and killed him.

My first appearance in court, if you see what I mean, led to another one of the occasions when I thought my journalistic career might be the shortest on record.

I tried to be very diligent and accurate in recording what was said in court. Then I put my copy in the basket next to the hatch into the subs' room. There soon followed the familiar cry from sub-editor Bessie of "Oh my God." She peered through the hatch at me. "Come here, boy." When I did so she brandished a piece of my copy.

The case I had written about was something like offending public decency. It was a different age when homosexuality was deemed not only immoral but illegal.

There were certain public conveniences in the Mansfield area where they met. I told Bessie that I had only written what was said in court about their activities.

Her tone softened. She said while that might be true, there were details that people did not want to be given over their breakfast on a Wednesday morning. A phrase like 'then the offence occurred' was quite enough.

Bessie's cry of "Oh, my God, what's all this crap?" was a daily occurrence and she had regular... er, lively debates with reporters about their stories. I soon decided that it was best not to argue with her but to keep my gob shut and try to follow her advice because it was worth listening to. For example, she told me that not every reporting job necessitated copy. Some parish council meetings, while maybe good for the local residents, were pretty boring and I would not be criticised if I did not waste time producing copy that would end on the metal spike as not worth using.

Donkey's years later, England were looking for a new football manager. I listened in my car to a sports bulletin on Radio Five Live. About 85 per cent of it was devoted to a league manager saying he had not applied for the job, had not been offered the job, did not know anyone who *had* been offered the job and he would not have taken the job had it been offered to him. "Where's the story, boy?" Bessie would have said.

I decided not to argue with Bessie, but once she left me speechless anyway. One evening he said something about an event, maybe the annual office Christmas meal. I pointed out that it was some way in the future and long before that my six-month trial period would be up and I might not be kept on to start my career proper.

"You shouldn't be worrying about that, boy." She said, gently, that I couldn't have worked any harder and my failings were down to lack of experience.

In turn I was gobsmacked, relieved and grateful.

I suppose I *could* have ended in court myself.

Reporters contacted the fire and ambulance services by phone several times a day to see if there was anything worth reporting. They were always friendly. The police station was close to the *CHAD* office so we visited three points of contact in the station: the general office, traffic and CID. The welcome we received varied markedly.

I was without a car one night and the last bus to Nottingham would be leaving shortly. I stood outside the general office. Several coppers were gathered in it and clearly saw me but just carried on chatting. I glanced at my watch, thought, "Bugger this," and went upstairs to the other offices before returning.

"Where the hell have you been?" a truculent copper asked. I explained. "You know damned well not to go up there until we tell you to," he said. "I'm not accusing you of anything but we've had quite a lot of stuff pilfered recently." I looked at him gobsmacked. Pilfering from a cop shop! I decided not to ask if they were on an efficiency bonus and made a dash to catch my bus.

Another time I went to the traffic office. The copper in that office had taken a break from collating details of traffic accidents, etc., and was deep in conversation with a pal. It was only the third member of that particular police force who saw my arrival at the office door and that was a police dog. A *big* police dog. He got slowly and deliberately up from his place near the radiator and looked at me as if he had decided to eat me without any bread. I managed to emit some sort of squeaking noise to attract the attention of the other two. The first copper told me there was no serious incident to report, the second one told his dog not to snack between meals and I escaped alive.

Then there was the time in court I nearly brought the house down.

The occasion was a 'not guilty' plea when there were plenty of witnesses to be cross-examined. Every time he had dealt with one witness the solicitor checked his paperwork and called out the name of the next one. Then he remembered that, due to illness, there was no court usher and he had to go to the waiting room himself to fetch them, passing the press bench to get there. Finally I took pity and signalled to him that I would do the errand.

As I rose from the back of the press bench my jacket caught my copy of the court list of defendants and it began to slide off the front of the bench. Frankly, I was poetry in motion. Without easing my pace and using all my cricketing skills, I caught the paper, one-handed, as it fluttered towards the ground and, in the same fluid movement, casually flipped it back into place on the bench. Then I walked into a partition!

I managed to get out of the courtroom while the glass pane in the partition was still rattling like a train, desperately hoping that the glass would not shatter where my shoulder had hit it. To continue the cricket theme, I'm sure that when I came back in with the witness my face was the colour of a well-polished cricket ball.

The glass had not fallen and all could have been well – except for the clerk to the magistrates. He told the court that members of the press were always valued for the work they did but the level of courtesy blah, blah, blah, blah, blaherty blah. This particular courteous but embarrassed member of the press sat there with a fixed half-smile while thinking: "For pity's sake shut your face."

I was not the only nutter in court. One of the solicitors could be relied on for a laugh, although usually between cases. However he was defending someone whose dog had been reported as a menace, driving the neighbours to distraction with barking. The owner said the dog only barked when tormented by the neighbour's cat which deliberately walked, safely out of reach, on top of the dividing wall. Postmen, binmen, kids – nothing else set the dog off.

"So," said the solicitor, "he'd go mad if I walked about near your garden in a cat suit?"

The magistrate in charge gave him a look. "That would send anyone mad, Mr Jones," she suggested.

Back to my pals, the Hell's Angels. I was sat in court when a mob of them were brought before magistrates. They were each charged with possession of a dangerous weapon. When police stopped them the Angels were wearing their 'uniform' of leathers and many had big belts with big chunks of metal in them.

The prosecution was going so well until the first one was asked why he had such a belt. The gist of the reply was in order to keep his trousers up! In fact, the trousers stayed up better than the prosecution case. Legally, at least at the time, an offensive weapon must be offensive per se and in itself, which a belt was not, or be used in an offensive way. The Angel had threatened nobody.

These days I often have secateurs in my car. Each pair has not one but two sharp blades that could do serious damage to someone's digits. Secateurs are designed for gardening and the only digits in danger, due to incompetence, are mine so that, i.e., QED and ipso facto, I could not be accused of anything illegal.

The first Angel got off the charge and there was no point in continuing with the other cases.

I tend to think some copper would have got into hot water, if not boiling oil, over the fiasco. Unless the whole idea was to make the Angels feel unwelcome in Mansfield in which case it probably worked.

I remember other cases with affection.

A police officer was giving evidence about seeing a

man with a loaded shopping trolley, pushing it over waste land in Mansfield, well away from shops. The copper was very sure that the stuff was nicked and gave his testimony clearly and precisely except... The magistrates had heard swear words before and needed to know exactly what defendants had to say. They asked three or four times for the copper to repeat the exact words, expletives and all.

Eventually the copper looked directly at the bench and, without stressing that it was the defendant speaking, he intoned, slowly and deliberately: "F... off, f... off, ... stick it up your arse."

It became a catchphrase in the office and was, perhaps, one of the defining moments in my career.

In another case it was the way that the story developed that I loved.

Our three brave lads, the defendants, were united by two things. One was a bellyful of beer. The other was that each had a new brain, each donated by a backward gnat.

Having supped mightily, they set out to the nearest Chinese restaurant. There they had a high old time abusing all the staff. This climaxed when the bill arrived. Having eaten everything that was put in front of them they proclaimed that they did not have to pay because the food had been crap. They would have said inedible but none of them could spell it.

The younger members of the restaurant staff were too well brought up and polite to quarrel too much. Luckily that did not apply to an older generation. When he heard of the problem, granddad emerged from the kitchen, waving a bloody great meat cleaver. Even in their befuddled state, the threesome managed to find the door pretty damned quick. They fled across the Market Place, pursued by granddad and his implement, and scooted up Westgate at a rate of knots. Hopefully after their exertions they puked up all the free food to which they thought they were entitled.

I don't know how many courses they had that night but, one way and another, they got their just deserts.

Your just deserts, dear reader, are apologies for such a lousy joke. Sorry.

5 Inky Noses and Computers

A GENERAL LINE of progression for newspaper reporters was to become a sub-editor, trying to ensure stories
made some sort of sense, were clear and hopefully had an
eye-catching headline. I said I would try the role because
it would be another string to my bow. The truth is probably that I fancied being in the warm more often.

Subbing was not so easy to get into because of the 'hot
metal' technicalities of newspaper production in those
days. In order to get something legible the paper rolls had
to come into contact with a mirror image so that left did
not become right. There's a game you can play by holding
a blank piece of paper over half a line of words on a book
or newspaper. You can easily detect what some of the
words are even if you are only seeing half of them. Others
not so much.

When you were subbing and went to the 'stone' where
compositors were assembling the type, you had to be able
to read the stuff upside down and back to front while
being suspended from the ceiling. Maybe I exaggerate just
a tad, but you get the picture.

When I moved to the *Leicester Mercury* to join their
subs desk I remember a sub called Charlie saying that he
would not be told what to do by any "inky nose." Charlie
was a perfectly amenable bloke and well liked, I'm sure,
by the 'comps'. But he was more experienced in his role
than me and could be more confident. I needed the comps'
goodwill and help initially. Later I was more relaxed and
simply enjoyed the banter and fellow feeling.

At Mansfield I had got to know some of the comps because their area was on my natural flight path between the tea machine and the gents' toilet. I thanked my late dad daily because I found a sense of humour invaluable and I believe I got it from him. It certainly helped the evening I had to go to one of my hated dinners. It was a posh do so I went to the gents to change out of my usual reporting gear and came out wearing a dinner jacket and all the other clobber.

On my passage past the stone I got orders for four gin & tonics, seventeen pints and an assurance that someone was on the way "to catch that bloody penguin."

The assistance and goodwill of a comp called Colin came to my aid on one occasion. A lad straight from school had been taken on as an apprentice. He was quite big lad and had a gob to match. We started off with banter between us but he developed from being too cheeky to a total pain in the bum because he never had the sensitivity to know when to stop.

Colin had a quiet word with me about the lad. He had told him that he should be more careful not to annoy me because, while I was not very big, I was a karate expert.

Next day I got waylaid by Colin and another old hand while walking through the comp room. They called over the lad who was still grinning and posturing but seemed slight less assured. Colin produced a solid piece of wood that was probably about five inches thick. Colin and the other bloke said, "Come on, Graham, show us all your party trick."

I was suitably reluctant and modest – all that stuff was a bit old hat. But they insisted and Colin held the wood in both hands in front of me. I paused, took a couple of deep breaths and chopped the wood into two imperfect halves with the side of my hand. The lad laughed but backed away and he was never as much of a problem to me again.

I had a quiet word with Colin a little later and thanked him. "Oh, that's OK, no trouble. Mind you, it took me ages to saw through that bit of wood. And it damned nearly fell apart twice before I could hold it out for you."

When I started subbing, I went to the stone with one of my early efforts at laying out a page. John the comp looked at the paper, pretended to wipe his bum on it and threw it over his shoulder. We both grinned and then got our heads together to come up with a page that fitted.

Thereafter he always greeted me with a big grin and I came to get along with him pretty well. Having said that, I still don't know why he insisted on addressing me as "Bombhead," but I figured it was best not to ask.

By that time the offices of the *Chronicle Advertiser* had moved from the town centre to Newgate Lane, maybe a mile away. The building backed onto the playing fields of a school. Subs and comps worked later on a Tuesday to prepare the paper for printing at Chesterfield next day. During a break at teatime some of us popped over a fence and played football on the field. If you had vexed one of the comps he would kick you up in the air the first time you went for the ball. After that all was forgiven. It worked well.

When I later moved to the *Eastern Daily Press* in Norwich, working from teatime to the early hours, I thought the comps, like many folks in Norfolk, seemed very laid-back. John was a Yorkshireman who called me "Petal" or "Peta-lini," Ian improved my pages and tried to improve my squash when we shared a court sometimes before work, and a younger bloke took to calling me "Duckie egg," which seemed an improvement on "Bombhead."

The comps included the head man John and his son Big Phil.

John was 90 per cent a lovely bloke. The 10 per cent

nobody appreciated was his flatulence. When anybody complained, his stock reply in his broad Naarfolk accent was "thaat hint nothing but a little puff of air."

His 'little puff of air' could have stripped three coats of varnish from a table. A cry of "'Look out, John's farted!" would send the entire crew scattering towards the nearest window.

Big Phil was a good comp. He once looked at a page and asked me if the picture would be better "on the huh." I looked at him blankly. He tilted the picture about 20 degrees. 'On the huh' was Naarfolkspeak for skewwhiff, and he was right, it did look better that way. While he was good, I think Phil would rather have been somewhere else. His mood usually improved after his evening break when he'd had a pint or several down his throat. I once accused him and another sub of swapping mucky films but then found it was classical music. Never judge a book... I gradually got to know Phil and felt I had really arrived one evening when he put a great bear paw on my arm.

"Graham, I've had too many drinks," he slurred. "I don't know what I'm doing so look after me and make sure I don't foul everything up." I promised to try.

A few years later I'm pleased to say that this male domain was invaded with one or two female comps, like 'Leafy' Elaine. She was very competent. I know it shouldn't have been a factor, but I was happier gazing into her eyes than the bloodshot orbs of Big Phil.

It was the days of unions and there were certain protocols to be observed. I liked the tradition of honouring retiring workers by bashing on the stone or tables as they left the premises for the last time.

The technical side of producing newspapers was changing dramatically over a fairly short time. At one time in the process we had a sort of hybrid system. Non-printers were never allowed to touch type but could send stuff through to the comp room. Sometimes you got the instruction wrong and so the type on a 'bromide' would not fit and it had to be redone. When I was promoted, or demoted, to be stone sub – the last line of defence before a page went away for printing – I learned always to carry a ruler. The comps would pick up and stick an offending effort on the ruler so I could correct it on a machine without actually making contact with printed material.

I got a life lesson from another comp on a day and evening when life generally was not on my side. The comp was complaining and asking why there was a particular problem which he would have to solve. I was past trying to think of some unlikely explanation. "It's because I cocked it up," I said.

He eyed me and then said "Well done. I'll always help anyone who will admit to a mistake." I can't claim I never blamed somebody else or the phase of the moon thereafter but perhaps not so often.

It honestly wasn't me that made one mistake but I almost wish it had been. A story that should have been in 7 point print (think roughly of an email today) was asked for in 72 point, the size of the biggest headline on a page – look on your computer. Apparently the comp seized the end of what should have been a little bit of paper and started to retreat, pulling it 10 feet, 20 feet, 30 feet from the machine, like unrolling a carpet.

Another placid character was Paddy. However, his language skills were limited. I think he was a graduate of the Billy Grozier school.

He instructed me to correct something to make it fit on a page. I walked some yards to the machine and luckily the noise around the stone had faded somewhat.

"Paddy," I bellowed. "Did you tell me to get on this fucking machine fucking quick and change the fucking type size so the fucking story fits in the fucking page?"

"Correct."

"Just checking."

The other comps enjoyed the exchange and my late Dad would have liked the humour but not the language. Even when he chopped off the top of his thumb on an unguarded machine he would not have used that word.

I never managed to strike up that same relationship of slight antagonism, but mixed with a goodly slice of humour, with computers. At one stage we had a lot of trouble producing a newspaper in Norwich because the computer system would roll over and die, risking wiping out hours of work in the process. The problem seemed to be lack of memory and I *can* identify with that these days.

Our company purchased a machine from Switzerland. As newspapers went along something like a dinosaur's back the machine would insert among their pages all the advertising flyers which are so common these days. Except it all went out of sync. I saw a photograph taken on the floor of the print room. There was a massive heap of advertising stuff which had been piled around one of the printers so there was just a pair of eyes visible, like something out of a cartoon.

When the redundancies started some of the comps left and others were moved to setting adverts. The jobs did not survive the changes in technology. So I climbed the stairs with a heavy heart one evening to shake hands with people like John, who was planning to go back to Yorkshire, and Ian. I just hope that they, like me, were eventually able to find happiness doing other things after redundancy. It was a privilege to have known them.

I can't say the same for the computer I used for the next few years. One evening, in particular, it was on a mission to thwart everything I tried to do. The next night I walked into work carrying a hammer. I turned on the computer, logged in and waved the hammer in front of the screen. "Any shit from you tonight and you get this," I explained. I had no problems.

The subs had a Christmas meal. The chief sub, Mark, must have spent hours preparing for the event. He organised it like an awards evening and prepared a personalised certificate for each of us. Mine was for "striking a hammer blow for freedom."

The same chief sub, however, was not so sympathetic to my next cunning plan. This was to work out which one computer was the most unco-operative, to unplug it and chuck it through the window. If these machines were so damned smart, then they would take the subtle hint and escape the same fate by behaving themselves.

I saw a recent suggestion that robots could provide companionship for people in care homes. If that is my ultimate destination then I can promise the robot provided for me a short conversation. A hammer will do most of the talking.

6 Transports and Delights

LOOKING BACK, I must have been fit as a flea in those days. Not only did I have youth on my side but I had no car. Rather than waiting around for buses, I used to walk for miles.

I often went out on jobs in a photographer's van and fellow reporters were generous in giving lifts. Tony was going out for a drink one evening with his pals. He suggested I could go in his car to The Hutt at Ravenshead (still a thriving business). I could then catch a Nottingham bus right outside the pub and save part of the bus fare. When we got to the pub it seemed only fitting that I should buy him a drink and have a swift half myself. Unfortunately, just as I was getting served his pals arrived. It would have been cheaper to get a bus ticket to Aberdeen.

There were advantages sometimes to travelling home by bus, like the chance to relax and then the conversation I enjoyed overhearing one evening. I was about to leave work when Jeremy arrived back from Chesterfield where he had checked the first papers off the press and he gave me a copy.

I boarded my bus. Two men were sat just behind me and their conversation went something like this.

Bloke A: "'Ere, he's got tomorrow's paper."

Bloke B: "You barmy bugger, how can it be tomorrow's paper?"

Bloke A: "I tell you it's tomorrow's paper."

Bloke B: "It can't be, it must be last week's, he must be a slow reader."

Bloke A: "It's definitely not last week's. I know what was in it and the stuff he's reading is different."

Bloke B: "It's the week before that's paper. He must be a *very* slow reader."

I should have done the right thing. I should have explained the situation to them, thanked Bloke A for being such a loyal reader and ceremonially presented him with a copy of the *CHAD* a day early.

Instead I let them watch as I got off the bus with a smug grin on my face and the paper under my arm.

I used to get off the bus in Arnold and take a stroll of 10-15 minutes to get home. Sometimes I and my dad would liaise about times and he would stick the dog in the back of the car and collect me to save me the walk.

Perhaps it was poetic justice. I got on the Nottingham bus without reading what was on the tin, so to speak, with the words Limited Stop under the service number. While I wanted to get off in Arnold the bus was not scheduled to stop until the centre of Nottingham. Dad and dog waited for me faithfully in Arnold. It was not easy to communicate with signals through the window of a speeding bus that I could not get off. Dog looked bemused and Dad looked somewhat annoyed. He continued to look annoyed and I joined him in a strop after having to catch another bus home from the middle of the city.

Another bus bafflement arose when I tried to cover a meeting of Cuckney Parish Council. For once it was not in the depths of winter but a balmy summer evening. I sat quite happily on the bus as it entered Meden Vale, then delighting in the name of Welbeck Colliery Village as I remember. Everybody else got off but I sat and waited for the bus to go on to Cuckney. Except that I had checked times correctly but not where that bus terminated. I told the driver that I had to get to Cuckney. He suggested that I could shorten the walk by taking a direct route.

I found the footpath and set off. The woodland would have been delightful normally. However, it was on top of a steep hill which I had been forced to climb and, despite a partial striptease, by that time I was pumping out sweat from every pore.

In the summer the council sensibly met in the pavilion In the middle of the cricket field. I reached the field and was 50 yards from the pavilion when the door opened and the council members filed out, meeting over.

My saviour was, would you believe, another ex-*CHAD* employee who, having heard my tale of woe and incompetence, put me in his car and took me back to Mansfield, while also filling me in on details and decisions from the parish council.

I learned a lesson – after a fashion. I had another parish council meeting to cover at Farnsfield and pored over the bus timetables.

My colleague Carole lived in Farnsfield and I asked if she knew much about the workings of the parish council, only to find out that her dad, a local businessman, was on it. She said the council meetings had a reputation for going on a bit and I said the last bus out of the village to enable me to get home left at 9pm.

Her reply was: "Well, if you miss the last bus my husband is away at the moment so I can offer you half a bed." I took it she said it in jest, but over the long years since I have been unable to stop myself wondering.

We had a young reporter with us fairly briefly and, if I'm honest, I can't remember his name. He was a bit taciturn but I did warm to him, in more ways than one, on one occasion.

He told me he was going for a night out with his mates in Nottingham and offered to save me bus fare by dropping me off. Fine, except that his transport of delight was a scooter and, of course, it was in the bleak midwinter. I was glad that he was quite hefty. It made the machine more stable as it buzzed like some monstrous mosquito between Mansfield and Nottingham and I was able to hide from the cutting wind. I got home more affluent and managed to escape hypothermia.

An old bike was the vehicle of choice for Trevor. He used to be the news editor but, from what I heard, was not a popular one. This was perhaps reflected in his sense of smell. He asked several reporters what was causing the terrible smell in the office. They all were trying not to gag but told him straight-faced that they could smell nothing unusual. It depends whether it was unusual for anyone to have a rotting kipper tied under his chair.

Trevor was a familiar figure around the courts and the football ground. We suspected his raincoat was so old that it moved on its own.

Trevor was the lineage king. Lineage was a system whereby you could supply copy to another newspaper and be paid, usually at so much a line. If you were in court and something interesting came up then you could try ringing one of the Nationals to see if they were interested. Harry once arranged for me to ring local radio with election results from the polling station at Newark and it was the easiest money I ever made, but generally I could not be bothered. Not so Trevor. He would appear part way through a court session and try to get details enough to scrape together enough cash for an unscheduled haircut. His comment amused us when he turned up late for a Mansfield Town A team match when the Stags lads were leading one-nil. He said he had heard the roar as he approached the ground. The crowd was sparse, to say the least. Maybe it was a combined yawn he heard.

I once went to his home with a query over something

he had written and he agreed to check on it. He sat me down with an egg timer and told me to keep count of how many times the sand in it had run out so that he could claim the right amount for the phone call on expenses. He continued in similar vein after I had left the *CHAD* until some idiot opened a car door without looking and knocked Trevor off his bike. He never really recovered.

I finally got a car but, of course, it did not solve all problems, although it did provide me with a portable office. It also helped with social occasions related to work.

There was one memorable journey home to Nottingham. It was certainly the worst fog I had driven in. I was at the head of a queue of traffic heading uphill towards the Larch Farm traffic lights at Ravenshead. The road has changed since then, of course, but I swear I left the road at one point, drove up the grass bank and several cars did the same before we all got back on the road. All was well and I felt a bit smug at the big roundabout at Red Hill. There was at least one car which had ended in the middle of the roundabout because they could not see where they were going. It then took me a minute to realise that the road was going downhill instead of uphill. I had driven all the way round the roundabout and was heading back towards Mansfield!

Again, events show how times change. I drove to the ground for a football match to find, to no one's surprise, that the gates were closed. It had been throwing it down all afternoon and the pitch was probably underwater. Near the entrance were two disappointed and very soggy young lads. I got them to jump in my car and dropped them at home before they drowned. Then it was the natural thing to do; today it might be treated with suspicion.

I once gave a lift home to one of our district correspondents who reported on small village events. She tried to help me by wiping off the condensation from the inside of the windscreen as we set off but dislodged the tax disc. Having dropped her off, I went back to the office.

On the way home quite late, I was stopped by the police. The outcome was that I was told I was not displaying my tax disk, a legal requirement in those days, and given a form to produce my documents at Mansfield police station.

Next day I had my documents with me but first covered a couple of cases at magistrates' court. A copper had to give evidence in one of the cases and, bugger me, it was the same one who had stopped me the night before. He had done his paperwork so, despite his apologies, I still had to present my form, etc.

Not even I could make it up.

Just when it felt that I was starting to settle into my role on the *CHAD* things suddenly changed. Les got the boot.

He had been having driving lessons and, like me, had been trying to save up for an old jalopy. He lived in Worksop where magistrates met one morning a week and Harry invariably put Les' initials against the job in the diary, giving Les a bit of a lie-in and saving on expenses.

For once Les probably forgot to check and the court either was not in session or Les was wanted in Mansfield for something else. Some of us did not consider it a sacking offence but the editor disagreed.

Prompted by other people, I suggested to Les that the union might be able to fight his corner but I got the impression he had already decided to try something or somewhere else.

I was sorry for him as a pal and sorry for myself, if I'm honest, to lose my mentor and because my workload immediately increased. It got very heavy because I no longer had anyone to share the obit notices and suchlike. It could have resulted in me following Les out the door.

Some people came into reception and asked why an

obituary had not gone in the paper that week. I should, presumably, have blamed 'production difficulties' but I was cheesed off and told the truth – I didn't have the time to do it. Luckily the truth paid off handsomely. Glenys was employed to work part-time to help with obits, weddings etc.

Not only was she very efficient but she was barmy and I began to look forward to the days when she was in the office. We were pushed in trying to keep up with things in the early part of the week but the pressure eased after publication day. We occasionally got cheesed off with all the wedding reports and made up our own. In our version, the bride dressed in string vest, tutu and size 8 Wellington boots and her father laughed with relief all the way through the service.

One day Glenys picked up that my phone call was to a pal, rather than business. She went into magician mode and began to tear paper with great showbusiness pzazz. I watched her out of one eye, expecting to see a chain of little paper men or a paper elephant emerge. Instead she took the bits of paper, opened a couple of buttons and stuffed it down my shirt.

I gave her a lift home one day and she asked if we could do a slight detour to pick up her daughter, Heather, from school. She was an angelic-looking little girl but not only pretty but pretty shrewd. Next day Glenys told me that Heather inquired why 'that man' had stopped himself from swearing in front of her. "Daddy never bothers."

Someone I was happy to meet at magistrates' court was a reporter from the *Notts Free Press* at Sutton-in-Ashfield called Chris. I got on with her from the start. Our relationship became another long one and we went to journalism college in Sheffield together. If we did not see each other for quite a long time we automatically seemed to just drop back into a comfortable understanding.

Once during a lull in court proceedings, she told me that she had heard I had got involved with someone in Nottingham. Otherwise she would have asked me to flat sit for her. She and her fella Guy were going to America for a few weeks. Guy loved to go climbing in his spare time, often in the Derbyshire Peaks. A crowd of them were venturing further afield and, of course, Chris was going with them.

I told Chris I was available. It struck me that, apart from the flat being much nearer to work, I was long overdue to start looking after myself a little instead of just letting my poor old mum, well, mother me.

I went to pick up a key and meet the slight complication. They had a little cat called Bruzz. This, I gathered, was very much a local word for nosey. How appropriate for an inquisitive young cat. He was quite barmy as well. Chris and Guy once set off from the flat in their car and noticed headlights flashed at them several times, even though they were only going a few hundred yards before pausing for petrol at their local garage. When they stopped the car they found Bruzz clinging to the roof.

He never repeated the feat for me but did try some other tricks. He didn't have a cat flap but used the open kitchen window since it was summer time.

He jumped in with a dead mouse in his mouth as a welcoming gift to me. I thanked him but opened the door at the front and chucked out the body. Within seconds Bruzzed jumped through the kitchen window with just the head in his mouth.

I also did some cat sitting for Roma. She and her husband John wanted to go away for a weekend but did not want to leave their two cats unattended. I drove round to their place to find a three-page epistle from Roma. I think the cats, we'll call them Cathy and Cuthbert, must have read it too because they acted just as Roma predicted.

Cuthbert gave me a look of disdain and then ignored me. Cathy was much more welcoming.

I later went upstairs and found her sitting on top of the balustrade. I did as instructed in Roma's notes and opened the door to the airing cupboard. Then I bent over and formed myself into a springboard for Cathy to land on during her flight into the cupboard, where she curled up in the warmth to sleep.

Cuthbert could read his script as well. When I went to bed he jumped up, decided I was OK after all and curled up with me, as he did with John, right between my legs. Maybe I'm a worrier, but the thought of well-developed claws being so close to my wedding tackle stopped me getting much sleep all weekend.

Roma was worried when I saw her back at work. She had fully stocked the freezer for my stay but I didn't mention that I dined elsewhere to save me much effort. She thought I had existed on cat-lit sandwiches all weekend.

John worked in some sort of time-&-motion study role and was offered some weeks of well-paid work in Pakistan. Roma was very nervous at the prospect of being alone in the house for all that time, particularly at night. John suggested that I should move in to keep her company. Roma ruled it out on the jolly old British objection of "What would the neighbours say?"

To this day, I still haven't worked out whether John trusted his wife implicitly and thought I was a man of great integrity – or maybe he thought I wasn't capable of misbehaving anyway.

Roma was obviously pleased to see John when he returned home because soon afterwards she said she was pregnant. She had car problems from time to time and I offered her a lift to an appointment. She and I got some strange looks as we subbed copy among the blooming ladies at a pre-natal class!

7 Death and Destitution

THE DAY I started on the *CHAD*, the body of Barbara Mayo was found dumped near the motorway in Nottinghamshire. My mum was worried that her wimp of a son would, on his first day, have to report on it, exam the body and perhaps conduct the post-mortem.

When you see journalists depicted in films they seem to fall into one of two clichés. Either there's a howling mob of them, beating on car windows and shouting questions at the victims of some tragedy or there's the brave hero, defying the power-crazed and death threats to get to the truth. I never fell into either category or met anyone who did. Maybe they only worked on the Nationals.

Death in accidents, inquests and obituary notices were, however, part of our stock in trade. The undertakers were phoned daily for names of the deceased and we took green forms to the families to gather information.

Bad (taste) joke alert. We rang the local crematorium too. The woman who answered the phone sounded quite mature but she had the sexiest voice, we all agreed. Talk about hot stuff!

A good part of the day-to-day work was taking out obituary forms and you tended to get a bit immune to some of it. I was at college with Big Nige (explanation later) who once remarked that his record was "Seventeen stiffs in a day."

Some of these jobs defied the ordinary. I was once let into a terraced house and shown into the living room, expecting to talk to one person about the deceased.

Instead I heard a cry of "I told you somebody would come from the *CHAD*." Kids seemed to come from everywhere and formed a semi-circle around me to watch proceedings. There was obviously nowt on TV that day. I felt a right let-down and heartily wished I had learned to juggle.

Most obituaries were for people who had hopefully lived a full and fulfilled life but news stories on accidents were different. I went to see a young woman whose husband had been killed in a crash.

She was obviously on the verge of tears but showed me into the living room of a nice home and excused herself for a few minutes. As I sat there the door opened and her two little daughters came in. They were too young to understand events and had been given cake or ice cream to keep them occupied. When their mother returned she found me on my knees trying to wipe away something spilled on one of their coats. How could you not be affected by the tragedy of the situation? I think the children went to Grandma while Mummy talked to me. It seemed she could keep her emotions in check while I, as a stranger, was businesslike, so that was the way I then tried to keep it.

Thankfully there were no fatalities from a fire in the midst of winter. I arrived at the house in the late afternoon when it had already grown dark. I bumped into a man wandering about the scene. He was the fire investigator and he invited me to join him in a tour of the property. The cold and dark made the whole experience memorable and spooky, especially when you contrasted it to the obvious damage which the heat of the flames had done.

A fellow reporter from the *Nottingham Evening Post* went to a similar fire scene and was allowed inside by the fire service. He asked about any casualties and was advised to mind where he put his feet.

My worst experience was in the wake of an accident, although to be honest I struggle to remember all the details. I think a young lad had been injured by a car. I do remember ringing the hospital and getting through to the intensive care unit for an update.

Many years later, before my mum went into a care home she had a phase of constantly being taken into hospital. Any attempt to check whether it was a panic attack or she was at death's door brought the answer, "We can't tell you anything over the phone, you'll have to pop in." The calls were made from Norfolk and the hospital was in Nottingham but that information was still met with 'pop in.' Some pop.

At this other extreme, a member of the nursing staff told me something like: "We haven't got anyone of that name now, he must have gone home." Later I thought perhaps I should have tried again because the message was somewhat vague.

The evening that we were going to press we learned that the child had died.

The family lived in the Annesley/Kirkby-in-Ashfield area and I remember the drive out to find the house. Again I was shown into a nice family home and invited to take a seat. I explained that the newspaper would appear the next day showing that their child was alive and well. I apologised profusely. The family could not have been nicer. They took the view that I had repeated what I was told by the hospital and it was somebody else's fault. I think even the family dog licked my hand.

I still drove away feeling pretty crap. This lovely family had been given the worst blow that anyone could receive and I had played a part in making their pain worse. Some folks would have been out for revenge.

One of the Mansfield characters of the time was an old fella who had a delightful way of 'mugging' people. He would approach with a broad smile, come to a halt like a sentry on duty, salute smartly and then put out his hand for any loose change.

Events in the *CHAD* reception were equally diverting and many hinged on the obituary reports, perhaps because people wanted to do justice to the memory of the deceased. If you missed out names from a list of mourners attending the funeral then trouble awaited.

I went into the bear pit one day to face a couple of large and extremely belligerent women, wanting to know why the obit and a list of mourners had been sketchy. I explained that I had been trying hard to get details with little success. In the end I had looked in the phone book and started to ring everyone with the right surname. I got through to one place where there was a lot of noise but it seemed to be a relative. A bloke was called to the phone and I explained again. He said yes, he was related but he had a pub to run and hadn't got the time to spare for all this stuff.

The first woman said, "Bloody Sid. Bloody typical." She looked at me and added, "Don't worry, meduck, it's not your fault, you did everything you could. Come on, Brenda, we'll go and have a word with our Sid now." I nearly rang Sid back to sell him my spare cricket box.

Another obit story was the old lad who was upset over the death of his old pal. Problem was that he had already been to a one-man wake. As I approached to try to help him I was met with fumes that nearly laid me out. I tried to work through the form with him but all I got, along with more fumes, was "He wash my pal," and "Washit got to do wiff you?" My patience was rapidly being exhausted.

Chief receptionist at the time was a lovely lady called Val who later became the editor's secretary. I think this was the first occasion that I noticed her nervous twitch. She said, "Graham, sorry to interrupt you, but there's an urgent phone call for you upstairs." There was a noticeable nod of the head and her left eye half-closed, almost like a wink. Val's urgent phone call and uncontrollable twitch got me out of many an encounter.

A regular plea to reporters in reception – but seldom successful – was for a court case to be kept out of the paper. Two young blokes came to me with the same plea. The actual defendant was polite and apologetic. I was equally polite but said he should not hold out too much hope.

His pal suddenly cut in. "It'd better not be in the paper or somebody's going to be bloody sorry," he said.

An aggressive voice asked him: "What the hell is that supposed to mean?" and the great surprise was that it sounded very like my voice. I had previously always taken the view that you could not beat a good dose of cowardice in such situations.

One time Ron went down to see someone who wanted to keep a court case out of the paper but he came back with a grin on his face. The woman had been charged with soliciting and had offered a free season ticket for him to do a little censoring of the news.

After I had left, Glenys worked in *CHAD* reception with a young woman called Carolyn, who became like a second daughter. This dynamic duo formed a double act that could deal with anything – until a bloke with a bandage on his hand walked in and told his tale.

It was almost like the old lady who swallowed a fly for those who remember the song.

> He wore the bandage,
> To cover the burn,
> Caused by the ray gun,
> In the grip,

Of the alien,
Who landed on the ring road,
To kidnap him

That's the way Glenys heard it but it was difficult to be sure over all the din. This was caused by Carolyn, behind a partition where she had fled, gasping and choking in an effort not to wee herself with laughter.

These days aforementioned Carolyn has a shedload of qualifications in psychology and suchlike and works as a mental health therapist. I kid you not.

Another, rather strange, incident was to do with planning applications. We used to check what plans had been lodged in a book in local council offices, in case anything merited a news story. The plan was for a hotel on Chesterfield Road, one of the main arterial roads into the town. The subs spotted that the application was lodged from an address which, we were pretty sure, was in a terraced street further out of town. I went to investigate.

It was, indeed, a terraced house and my knock on the door was answered by a young, well-groomed man. He confirmed all the sparse details we had so far but explained that the project would be financed by a company in London which was using his address. He would love to give me complete details further down the line but for the moment was sworn to secrecy and would have to discuss it only in the broadest terms.

Shortly thereafter I received a phone call from the head of Mansfield CID, asking me to go and see him at the police station. He was one of the informative local coppers and had once been good enough to give me a lift to work when he had seen me a bus stop in Nottingham.

He knew all about my enquiry concerning the planning application. He also knew about the young man involved and we agreed how pleasant and plausible he was. The fact that he was *so* plausible made this copper's life more difficult. Several times a month he was forced to see people like me because chummy was being treated for mental illness and constantly coming up with unlikely tales. My policeman friend said he could not and would not interfere if I wanted to do a story but hoped I would take the tip-off on trust. Which would anyone believe?

The legal position, by the way, was that you were allowed to put in an application to build the Eiffel Tower in Mansfield Market Place – getting planning permission was another matter.

I also developed a trusting relationship with Harry. As news editor, he was the first to get hauled into the editor's office if something had gone wrong. Invariably when I was the culprit I would walk past Harry on my way to be interrogated. Harry would whisper out the corner of his mouth, "Tell him…" so we had the same excuse ready.

My return favour to Harry was to do with cotton wool. The feel of the stuff used to give him the screaming abdabs so I had to remove copious amount of it from the keys of his typewriter where some sadist had draped it.

Harry had two sons who followed him into journalism. I loved one story about his youngest, Chris.

To save the cost of renting a flat Chris had a tiny caravan. It also saved him on travel expenses because it was parked in Newark, not too far from the newspaper office. His mates decided that he had been working hard and deserved a good night out. To cut a long story short, he had a skinful and woke the next morning with a pounding head. He put the kettle on to brew some black coffee and stepped out of the caravan door. It was a lovely vista that met him of fields and woodland. The only problem was that he hadn't a clue where he was. While he was sleeping off all the booze, his mates had hooked up the caravan to the back of a car and driven it off into the wilds!

The older lad, Harry junior, was concerned about money in a different way. He volunteered as a leader of adventure scouts and was trying to raise funds for them. The answer was for a sponsored event of a new kind. The lads would be sponsored for a 24-hour event that I would call a 'cave-in'. They would descend under the Derbyshire countryside and stay there until the time was up.

For once I had been forewarned that I would be going with Rog to do a feature about it and had taken an old coverall thing to wear. Trouble was that the entrance into the underground complex was a hole made by an under-nourished rabbit. As I slid down into it my top was pulled up and my decent shirt was covered with some soil, which would easily clean off, and grass stains, which would not. When I tried to make an expenses claim it made for something of a battle.

The gulf between the experiences of junior reporters and executives was shown by a memo we received about expenses. In particular it involved my bête noire of attending dinners. The memo said they were part and parcel of a reporter's experience and so we should all have our own dinner suits. Right, on reasonable but not excessive pay rates, we could all afford to have posh suits, bow ties, etc., hanging in our wardrobes for the couple of occasions each year that they might be needed.

I suppose an expenses claim for a new duck house was a bit excessive.

The vast majority of dinners were for companies, and for the employees attending a decent suit was quite adequate. Previously we had been permitted to claim for hiring a dinner suit.

A friend to people at the *CHAD* was Reg Strauther, a local tailor who became county council leader. I went to him when a posh dinner was looming and he took my measurements to send for a hired penguin suit. I checked several times and it was on its way.

The day before the dinner I went to Reg's shop and the damn thing had still not turned up. Reg, bless him, said to come back the following day and he would loan me his one. The jacket could have been made for me – not the trousers. I went to the dinner with every tissue and piece of rag I could find stuffed in the pockets and a really tight belt round the waist. Good job I was only called on to write and not to dance as I could have been arrested.

Sometimes the memorable days are those you would rather forget, if that makes any sense. I arrived for work one Friday knowing that I faced a long afternoon.

The local coroner was based in Nottingham. He would only venture into the wild and lawless north occasionally and waited until there were at least half a dozen inquests for him to deal with. It always got to me at the conclusion when the 'good men and true' of the jury were invited to "Go forth and take your ease," or something along those lines. *It's all right for them,* I thought, *I've got to go back to the office at tea time and start to write up all this lot* – unless there was a chance to start scribbling during a pause in proceedings.

The coroner was none too popular among reporters. Rumour had it that he had a long-running feud with the press over something and he conducted inquests in little more than a whisper, so we always had to check details from the copper who was coroner's officer.

The coroner had a soothing phrase for relatives about "an old engine wearing out." We reckoned he would use it if the poor deceased had been hit by the 8.30 express train to Edinburgh.

I did not have long to dwell on the thought of inquests this particular day. Ron could not report for duty because he was ill. Visits down pits were plentiful in a mining area, as Notts was in those days, and anything to do with the National Coal Board was worth covering so someone would have to take over. No prizes for guessing…

The consolation would be that the NCB always put on a very good buffet after any event and journos could usually be relied on to do an impersonation of vultures at a kill. Except…

The night job for Harry was a Burns Night Dinner for which a dinner suit was required. But Harry, too, was ill.

I went down the pit until lunchtime and then I went to the inquests until tea time. I went back to the office and bashed out reports of the inquests as fast as I could. All I then had to do was to nip round the corner to the Co-op building, give our apologies due to unforeseen illness, blah blah, arrange to ring someone for details about the Burns Night and then head for home.

As I climbed the stairs to the Queensway Suite, where many a dinner celebration was held, I heard the strains of what I assumed was traditional Scottish music. The name Graham is the only link I have to anything remotely Scottish. I had never tasted haggis, been to the Highlands or milked a set of bagpipes, let alone was up to quoting Rabbie Burns. I did, however, like the lilting tones of the man who came to take my apologies. Seems to me that some Scottish accents are harsh on the ears but others are musical. This bloke was definitely musical.

I tried to give him my tale of woe but he and his wife were having none of it. I won't attempt to do the accent because I would hate to insult anyone. They said a place at the table was already set for a *CHAD* representative and, after all my rushing about, I could probably do with a good feed. They had a proud tradition of making people welcome even if, like me, their legs were most unsuited for a kilt and It did not worry them one jot that they were dressed in their finest while I was remarkably ill-equipped for decent company. Bugger – why, oh why did they have to be so damned nice?

I can now say that I *have* tasted haggis and I found it OK while the rest of the fare was pretty good. The atmosphere was warm and welcoming, but it did not alter the fact that I knew no one. The other problem was that there seemed to be multitude of traditions connected with the occasion and they took so long.

I suspect there are also local variations on the theme – like piping in the haggis. I swear that, while I was trying to keep a low profile, male guests at this occasion were invited to greet the centrepiece of the feast not just with applause but by standing with one leg on the table and the other on their chair. It felt like a week had elapsed before I could take a shorthand note of the speeches, check the names and flee to the office.

The Queensway Suite had a good reputation as a dinner venue, both for the food and the beautifully clean and pressed table linen. I just have a nasty suspicion that when staff cleaned up after this particular event they could tell the exact place occupied by the *CHAD* reporter. There was probably a thin layer of coal dust left on the tablecloth.

Then there was a better day for us all. I went off to the council offices again to get the latest list of planning applications.

The atmosphere when I left the office was as normal as we ever got. When I returned it had changed to carnival. People were standing around or sitting on desks, everyone talking at once.

"What the hell is going off?" seemed to be the obvious first question.

Tony jerked a thumb in the direction of the editor's office. "He's gone."

"What?!" seemed to be the obvious second question.

Tony explained that our not-so-esteemed editor had

come into the main office, shaken Harry by the hand and said something about the pleasure of working with him and, like Elvis, left the building.

It later transpired that he had had trouble getting along with other members of the board as well as those of us who were further down the food chain and it had resulted in a swift exit.

Everybody else that day seemed to have a hot drink in hand so I went to the machine. What I got looked and smelled like tea but it tasted to me like champagne.

The next day I was back to the normal run with cups of coffee and tea on my little tray. I took the last drink to the editor's office, knocked on the open door and waited on the threshold.

"What are you buggering about at?" asked Jeremy, not very grammatically.

I explained that he was now the (acting) editor so the situation was different.

"I'm still Jeremy," was the reply. Luckily he was not merely acting editor for long; they had the sense to confirm the appointment pretty promptly.

8 Foreign Fields and Twin Towns

SO, WHEN I was called on to do my bit and report on local soldiers who had joined up to keep the Red hordes at bay, did I set off intrepidly? Did I hell. I set off looking for someone to hold my hand and get me through it.

The brief, such as anybody spelled it out, was to talk to squaddies from our circulation area currently in Germany with the 1st Royal Horse Artillery.

Apart from a very early start, the whole thing began well with a rail journey down to London. I was to report to an Army recruiting office down t'Smoke and it was there that I thought the hand-holding might begin. Instead I was given a load of paperwork and put on a bus to Luton Airport. It seemed a long journey round the sprawl of London.

It was to be the first time I had flown and I was full of trepidation. As always, it seemed a very long process to check in and get through customs, perhaps made longer because the flight to Dusseldorf was with the Ministry of Defence.

If I thought I was a bit twitchy it was as nothing to the young woman sat in the next seat. Not surprisingly she was German, judging by the magazine she was holding. I was going to say reading, but her hands were shaking so much that she could never have focused on the text.

As the aircraft thundered down the runway and took to the skies I deliberately caught her eye. I was not sure that my O-level German conversation skills were up to a message of "Relax, I fly several times a week and it's all a piece of cake," but there was no need as I said it all with a warm smile and a suave expression. However, at that point it felt as if the bottom had dropped out of my seat and I made a panicky grab at the arms. I gathered later that there are houses quite close to Luton Airport. It was policy for pilots to throttle back the engines as soon as possible to keep the noise down. This might stop them blowing a hole in anyone's eardrums but it also blew a big hole in my show of bravado.

After landing in Germany and getting through customs, I finally found someone to hold my hands – or rather several of them. I found myself in a minibus with a group of squaddies who were returning to barracks.

Their presence was reassuring and they were friendly but their conversation was not comforting.

The regiment was taking part in 'manoeuvres' or war games and my new pals gave me tips about not adding me to the list of casualties. The idea was to re-enact war conditions, so evenings and night time could be perilous. There were a great many heavy vehicles moving about without lights showing and you had to keep your eyes open and your wits about you. It was not as easy as that sounds because the people driving those vehicles might be somewhat knackered and could sometimes nod off to sleep.

I'm not sure how popular these events were with the locals. While they were perhaps comforted by an allied force to stop any Red invasion their countryside was ploughed up considerably.

The lads I was going to join were in Abbot Guns. They were four-man track vehicles, like smallish tanks. Apparently the drivers tended to test their skills, and keep boredom at bay, at road junctions. They could flip the back end round and aim to clip a road sign, sending it cartwheeling out the ground.

Rather than roughing it, my stay started with the height

of luxury. My first night was spent in the commanding officer's bed. Luckily, for both of us, he was not in it. Also I had my own 'batman' while the boss man was out in the field with the rest of the regiment.

Again, I was treated with friendly words and caring thoughts. Once, my pal Martin and I went searching for a scenic waterfall in Scotland – or was it the Lake District? We wore our usual outfits of jeans and trainers and were told by a woman and her pedant of a husband that we were "remarkably ill-equipped" for the task.

This evening I got the same look from my batman. I said I had not been given a clear picture of the conditions I would be facing, which was why my usual old raincoat was doing service. Bless him, he woke me next morning with a cup of tea and a pair of his own boots so that I was at least well shod.

Breakfast was a quiet affair because while there was plenty to eat there was only a handful of people left on the base.

I eventually managed to link up with the unit I was meant to be visiting. Apart from playing 'smash the road sign', they quite enjoyed pass the parcel and this time the parcel was me. I was passed from one Abbot gun to another so that I met as many of the lads as possible.

Now let me share with you my technical knowledge of Abbot guns – they were like 17-tonne dustbins. That's the way it felt to me when I travelled in one, and over the next couple of days I travelled in one a lot. They were designed to do a particular job of work and, understandably, were built for conflict, not comfort. Perhaps the worst aspect was the noise from all that metal getting bashed about over road and field.

The Army continued to try to give me a degree of comfort but, understandably, business came first. That's partly why I only took off my boots when I was shown to the camp bed they had provided for me. I heard the radio crackle and asked if I had better get up. "Hang on a minute," was the reply but it was followed shortly afterwards by "Sorry."

The scenario, I guessed, was that the unit was to move once the position of the enemy had been identified and then to find the best spot from which to send armaments.

Anyway, I was soon in the back of an Abbot gun again, sitting against the side. It was not too claustrophobic but most of the room was taken up by the gun turret - and that kept moving. I felt a bit like a pair of old Y-fronts in a washing machine. I had to retreat round the edge every time that the turret approached. I just hoped it wouldn't go into fast spin cycle. After a short while I decided the role of dirty laundry was not much fun so I jumped out of the door at the back on the next circuit.

Again the squaddies tried to help. One told me to see Terry, get a sleeping bag from him and kip down on top of the engine, which would still be warm from all the travelling about. I did as advised and found that the last sleeping bag had gone – Terry had taken it, settled down on top of the engine and was fast asleep. I decided not to disturb him out of the warmth of fellow feeling and the fact he might have killed me.

It's a cliché to talk about the longest night of my life but this was certainly in contention. There's no subtle way to give the climactic information, sitting on a tank in a German field, in the middle of winter it was flippin' freezing.

I got through the time by hopping around the gun and stamping my feet to get a little warmer and then going back to the best place to keep out of the wind. The other way to pass some time was to ponder on the vital questions, like why the hell can't they defend the sovereignty of Germany during the summer, for crying out loud?

I like the name Dawn. I liked the sight of it even more on the following day.

I was not greatly surprised to find that I had failed the audition to be the right material for a Tommy. As I awaited breakfast, I saw several of the lads I had met, whistling merrily as, stripped to the waist, they washed in cold water.

Another tip I had been given by the squaddies I had travelled with initially was never to turn down food because you didn't exactly have set meal times while on manoeuvres. For breakfast I had the best meal of my time in the wilds and I began to feel that life was looking up. Then I was moved to see another Abbot gun crew and given another breakfast.

Shortly afterwards I was given a turn with one of the battalion's toilet rolls. I had been in enough changing rooms for squash and cricket that I was not excessively shy but this was different. There were plenty of woods about but there were also lookout posts. I set off for the trees and kept going for quite a long way, overly conscious that eyes might be watching me. I found a good enough tree for doing my dog impersonation but, without being too graphic, let's just say that no self-respecting bear would have welcomed me into the family.

The squaddies were very apologetic to me that I would be missing all the fun. The plan was for their precious Abbot guns to move on by 'swimming' across a river. They had done this before and were very enthusiastic. I hadn't and wasn't. My habit of thinking of the guns as dustbins probably did not help. Dustbins leak. I was quite happy, thank you very much, to wish them all the best and head back to the barracks and then to the airport.

I had time at the barracks to add another memory. It was the face of my batman when I handed back his crap-encrusted boots. I had done my best, in the time available, to clean them up but he still had much work to do. I felt like an ungrateful bounder.

I arrived at the airport and reported to a desk, clutching

all my travel documents. I was told that it was too early for me to check in luggage and so found a quietish corner to sit and wait. I returned to the desk later to be given the same advice.

I'm normally OK with my own company but sitting in that airport lounge was one of the loneliest times in my life. Everybody else seemed to be travelling in groups or at least pairs. Time dragged.

On another attempt to check in, I found a bloke who seemed to be in the same situation. The staff seemed as baffled as he and I were until the penny dropped with someone. "You've not been on trips with the Ministry of Defence, have you?" We both confirmed it. "Oh, their check-in desk is on the other side of the airport."

We got to the designated check-in spot. Was this the right place and could we please check in our luggage? Yes, it was the right place, but no, we could not check in our luggage. The flight was still on the ground but there was not enough time for everything to be processed. My companion, called Jim, had not been delivered to the airport at the right time and I had not been delivered to the right place.

After lengthy conflabs, we were to be given more documents – these ones for rail travel to a port and tickets for an overnight Channel ferry.

I spent some of the waiting time spending a chunk of my German currency in a booth to make a telephone call to my parents, telling them I would not be home until the next day. I asked my mum to ring the *CHAD* news desk to tell them of the problem. She was asked what time I would arrive at the office because there was a list of jobs on tomorrow's diary with my initials against them. I believe she said what I would have said in those circumstances – without the expletives.

I found Jim and we had a chat about our experiences. He said he had really enjoyed his time with the Army, had been well fed and watered and was especially enthusiastic about a helicopter flight.

There was just time before our train left to use some more of my currency and my superb language skills at a stall in the station. By this time I was pretty hungry and I wasn't sure what facilities there would be on the train. I invited Jim to dip into my paper bag from the fruit stall. He said he was quite replete with food. I wished I had remembered that the German words for apple and cooking apple were different. I suspect my face gave away what I had done.

When we got on the ferry, Jim seemed disappointed that I was reluctant to do much exploration of the craft. All I really wanted was a quiet spot because my reserves of energy were pretty depleted. Jim was even more disappointed with me later. I thought he had told me that he was married but he seemed quite excited by a pair of young women he had been talking to. His problem was that there were two of them and he wanted me to engage one in conversation, presumably the one he did not fancy. I'm not sure that my chat-up routine was ever particularly good, and certainly not after a few days with little rest. Jim was probably glad to see the back of me when the ferry docked in the morning.

There are times when some things seem inevitable. As I pulled my case towards customs I saw one of the officers looking in my direction and just knew I was about to get picked out.

I began to undo the straps on my case as he asked me where I had been, how long for and what I had bought while there. He grinned at my reply and readily agreed that retail opportunities were limited on top of a tank in the middle of a German field. He told me to shut my case again and "Get off home." I was happy to comply.

The net result of all this was that I did a feature for the paper that seemed to pass muster.

Then I had one of *those* conversations when approached by Tony, asking me for the sidebar, or subsidiary story, quoting all our local heroes.

"Most of the squaddies were from Nottingham or parts south," I said.

"So how many were from our circulation area?"

"One."

"One! Did you talk to him?"

"No."

Long silence. "Why not?"

"I couldn't shout that loud..." My turn for a silence. "The day before I got there he shut his hand in an armoured door and was carted off to hospital 30 miles away."

People can challenge my religious beliefs but they will never convince me that God has not got a lively sense of humour.

After that triumph, it was only fitting that I should be called back to Germany. The *CHAD* was involved in quite regular visits to local serving soldiers, but they were mainly by the winner of the Miss Sherwood Forest competition and I only came third.

This trip was to do with town twinning where places like Mansfield established links with other communities in other countries. I was all in favour of the idea of helping towards mutual understanding. As a species, Man seems to feel superior, claiming great intellect. If that's the case why do so many either attack others or build barriers to keep out folks who have the nerve to wear socks of a different colour?

I well remember a story about my visit, probably with the Army, to a small German village where a woman and her mother lived in houses within a couple of hundred yards from each other. The problem was that the border between East and West Germany came through the middle of the village. They were able to stand in bedroom windows and share a surreptitious wave with each other. But if they wanted to share a cup of tea one or the other would need to get a train to Berlin, cross through the Brandenburg Gate or similar and then get a train back to the village – to arrive back virtually where they started. I'm not the smartest member of the species so perhaps some clever clogs could explain the sense in that to me.

My summons back to Germany was with a collection of people from Mansfield council. The idea was that contacts built up with individuals and clubs at a place called Heiligenhaus should be formalised with the signing of an official twinning document. For once, party politics would be put to one side as the delegation would include both Conservative and Labour councillors, with a senior officer going to ensure there was no fighting in the playground. The signing would be done by the chairman of the council. I would witness and write about the whole event.

As you will have twigged by now, my memory is not always so reliable. It let me down in this case because I forgot to tell our dear readers about the trip to the airport. Some ratepayers would perhaps have raged to know that the council chairman's official car was used, complete with chauffeur. He was the one who urged discretion on me. Frankly it made sense to me. Half a dozen people had to get on the same plane at the same time and rail travel or similar would have been a real exercise in logistics. Maybe we should have used a mini tank.

One of the people on the trip was Labour councillor Gladys Pidduck and she immediately dubbed us the Quality Street Gang, like the assorted chocolates, as we piled into the council limo. Not only would I not have to travel in a rattling dustbin but I would get a hotel bedroom in Heiligenhaus. Luxury.

The flight and trip in general was much less fraught than my earlier experience, and the gang seemed to get

along pretty well. I felt I was treated just like the councillors by the friendly German officials and I still have an
ornament, used as a bookend, in the shape of a stirrup.
They were given as prizes at a gymkhana we attended.
OK, I didn't get a clear round but neither did I drown at
a rowing race or kill anyone when we were invited to try
our hand on the local club's rifle range.

We were also shown a local council housing scheme
which was one of the things that made these twinning
ventures so valuable. Our councillors were able to see how
people were housed in another country, and Mrs Pidduck
demonstrated another value. We entered an apartment
where an elderly couple were living. The German hosts
included several people who spoke excellent English and
they interpreted. This time they were not needed as Mrs
Pidduck just gave the old lady a big hug that needed no
words.

The only way that my schedule varied from the official one was that I was to be taken to the local newspaper
office while the rest of the gang had a flight over the town.
When we got to the landing strip and I saw how flimsy the
light aircraft looked I was quite pleased to be missing out.
I decided I preferred a solid airliner around me. Added to
that was the fact that a large power cable was strung right
across where the grass runway seemed to be.

Getting all the councillors to see Heiligenhaus from the
air would take several flights so people started to have
their seats delegated, while I looked around for the car
that would take me to the newspaper office. Then somebody piped up, "What about Graham?" I said I would have
reluctantly to pass because of the time but the answer was
that the newspaper was quite near and I could be squeezed
onto the first flight.

I did not realise how appropriate was the expression.
I got into the back of the little plane, along with Tim
Martin, one of the Conservative councillors who was

about my build. In the front seat was our council chairman, eventually. He was not very mobile, shall we say, and must have weighed about 18 stones. It took several attempts to get him aboard, and I was convinced that the wing would not take the strain of him standing on it. We three waited for several minutes until the pilot emerged, clutching his flight plan or whatever. He could give the chairman a couple of stones!

The engine came into life and sounded to me like a worn-our lawnmower. The little craft started to scoot and bounce over the grass and, by this time, I was convinced would never be able to leave the ground. It did so – and headed straight towards the power cable. It climbed to go above the cable but then the pilot throttled back to put us back on a collision course. Under or over? I do not know but when I opened my eyes we were clear of it and, somewhat to my surprise, after that I enjoyed the ride and the aerial views.

After landing, not only did I still have time for my visit but I even got back to the hotel before the others. In the sanctuary of my room I realised that I would have plenty of time for a freshening shower before we were to gather in the entrance hall and be taken to the signing ceremony. Unfortunately the time I was given was wrong. Luckily I was just about dressed and ready when another councillor, Jim Hawkins, came bashing on my door to say get a move on or we would miss the ceremony. I'm not sure the newspaper would have been too pleased had I missed the main event.

After an interesting and worthwhile few days were headed for home – in a nice *big* plane.

The flight was fine until we approached touchdown. I was sat next to Mrs Pidduck and she told me this was the part that made her nervous, especially as it was grey and raining and you could not see the ground. I did my casual flier impersonation which had been such a previous success and held her hand.

How strange. If either of us had known then that we would one day become mother-in-law and son-in-law perhaps he or she would have thrown themselves out of the plane anyway!

9 Seats of Learning and Perishing Politicians

THE LONG-TERM AIM was to get a proficiency certificate from the National Council for the Training of Journalists. You could do it in one go by attending college full time but I'm glad I went, largely by chance, the other route. Having got through the initial trial at the *CHAD*, I was signed up to attend Richmond College in Sheffield for spells of a few weeks in consecutive years. Best of all, the courses would be in summer, making travel easier and the whole experience more enjoyable.

I drove up to Sheffield one Sunday and checked into the hotel which *CHAD* reporters had traditionally used. The hotel was fine and my room was comfortable but I was still relieved in the morning to walk into the dining room for breakfast and reunite with my pal Chris. In a world full of strangers, I would have one friend and supporter at least.

The first other reporter I met who would be on the same course delighted in the name of Richard Cox. As someone pointed out, Dick Cox was a bit like a double negative.

There were two or three floors to the hotel but also a basement space where there were two rooms, a single and a twin-bedded room. Chris had already taken possession of the single, but Dick was alone in the twin-bedded room. He invited me to join him. I was dubious about sharing, not being very sociable, but he had a big point in his favour. The room was cheaper than those upstairs and the manager was quite happy to fill out paperwork showing I was still in a more expensive room.

There will now be a pause, dear reader, before I bring my tale to an end to allow for me being arrested by HMRC or the Fraud Squad for fiddling expenses... OK, the coast seems to be clear.

When we got to college, there was a mixed bag of boys and girls to share the adventure, and consistently three lecturers, Ron, Frank and Jerry, to deal with subjects like writing styles, grammar, newspaper law and local government. Brain surgery for beginners had ceased to be on offer.

There was a contingent of folks from the wilds of North Yorkshire and they rapidly formed the heart of group. There was a bloke called Nigel and he became Little Nige to distinguish him from Big Nige. Not that there was much chance of mixing them up. When we got into discussions, Little Nige expressed political views that seemed slightly to the right of Attila the Hun. Big Nige was big and bluff. He must have weighed about 17 stones, played Rugby League at weekends and also had a forthright attitude, grounded, I considered, in a no-nonsense, working-class-type approach, proud of his birthright.

The dark side of life made its presence felt later in the first year. Big Nige was driving his gang home on Friday and a tyre burst on his car. One lad, Leigh, was just about scalped and his girlfriend was injured, thankfully not as badly. They were later able to return to the fold. The group was made more united by the accident and we were even more supportive of Big Nige. We suspected that he felt even worse because, while his friends were injured, he walked away unscathed. When he was asked what had happened he replied with the single word: 'Remoulds." There for the grace of God, because most of us had tried to save money on car parts.

My gang of two with Chris became a gang of four.

It was all very confusing because my pal Big Chris was joined by Little Chris and David. Again, the confusion was in name only because Little Chris was definitely a fella and quite a character. Long before the recent trend, he had an earring. He had gone out with a girl from a travelling family and had a hole put in his earlobe as some form of welcome to the community.

We didn't know if he still saw the girl because, little, bright and bouncy, he seemed to cut a swathe through the female population of Derbyshire where he lived. He could drive to Sheffield each day, rather than live in a hotel, and had a habit of turning up to college in a different vehicle each week.

We once had an outing to Lincoln in two cars and I drove one which I had borrowed. I warned Little Chris, who was following in one of his array of cars, that the handbrake in mine did not seem very tight. Since we had to climb the hill approaching Lincoln Cathedral I did not want him too close in case my clutch control was not good enough. Little Chris had his driver's car window open. "Handbrake a bit ropey, is it?" He asked. "Try this one!" and he handed me the one that sat between his front seats, not attached to anything.

The madness of youth.

David, quite a laid-back character, at least on the surface, was staying in our hotel, where others from the college sometimes gathered. Some years later he and his wife emigrated to Canada and he embraced his new country wholeheartedly. It proved good for me too because I scrounged a memorable holiday to Edmonton one summer. He and his wife number two said that most of the kids in their fused family were going to summer camp and they could accommodate another kid, namely me, for a couple of weeks. The Rockies were great and the grizzlies didn't get me.

Of course, you'll believe all of us were devoted to our studies and never went into pubs but, changing times again, I remember feeling more anti-social than ever because I didn't smoke when everybody else seemed to be handing round the fags.

One bloke had a clever party trick. He had had some form of accident, maybe playing sport, and had damaged his jaw. He could pop it out of place and grind out 'Twinkle, twinkle little star' on it. Tall, blond and handsome, he seemed popular with the female members of our brave bunch, but he did not return to college for a second year like the rest of us. We heard that he had been allocated to a branch office of his newspaper and opened the door regularly – about once every two months.

Of the lecturers, Ron was lively and Frank was a stickler for grammar but, once you got to grips with is old-school attitude, gave valuable guidance.

Jerry was an excellent lecturer and a brilliant musician but also an all-round good egg, unassuming and modest.

By coincidence, he told us one Monday of an incident that had happened to him and his family over the weekend. After doing some shopping, they returned to find their vehicle isolated in a car park and surrounded by dozens of motorbikes. Like me, he approached the Hell's Angels types with some trepidation. He asked politely if they could move their machines so he could drive his car out. The said not a word but complied OK. But then, they did not invite him to a local hostelry to buy him a drink...

Despite the reputation, we students did some studying at the college and in our hotel rooms, probably ending the evening with a drink in the bar. I said one time that I might not make that late drink as I wanted to wash my hair, like a prim prima donna. The room door flew open later and David and Big Chris steamed in. David got busy filling the wash basin with hot water and Big Chris got me out of my shirt before proceeding to wash my locks for me – an altogether pleasurable experience.

Mixed in with the regular journalism lectures there was others about wider affairs or somesuch. We had to travel to another college and the lecturer was a young woman who was pleasant but not really on the same wavelength as us journos. We soldiered on until one day when the sun was blazing down and the Gang of Four decided that we could not face her lecture. We found a pub for something to eat and a refreshing drink. I was behind the other three and faithfully followed on the end of the crocodile that filed into the pub corridor, into one room, out again and into a second room, Little Chris leading the way.

When we had each got a sandwich and a drink I asked Little Chris the reason for the guided tour of the premises. "Did you see those rough-looking blokes in the first room? They looked up at me and told me to fuck off, so I fucked off." Fair enough.

There were changes from year one at the college to our second spell, which would eventually lead to qualifying exams. We each had to do some sort of project after the first spell at college and I chose to write about the pressures on the Sherwood Forest area, with tourism greatly helping the area but risking the environment due to all those tramping feet. Then, as now, some people looked at the forest and glades and saw not scenes of beauty but pound signs.

I arranged to meet the Head Ranger to learn about the issues and he was very informative, when I could hear what he was saying. This was made somewhat difficult by the snoring sounds coming from his old dog, curled up in the corner.

It's maybe a stretch, but I was reminded at one point of my fears of taking off in a light plane in Germany. The Ranger had taken me out in his Land Rover for a mini tour of some of the areas under discussion. We were headed for quite a narrow gap between a couple of trees. I'm sure he was an accomplished driver but the situation was made more complicated by the aforementioned dog. He had woken up, livened up and wanted to get out of the vehicle to investigate all the scents he had picked up. He thought it was a good time to paw at his dad's forearm on the steering wheel. I didn't.

I had joined the National Union of Journalists quite early on and I believe mentioned that we urged Les to call on the union over his sacking. The 'chapel' of union members was not large. The person who liaised with the employers was called the 'father of the chapel' and we lost ours when someone moved away. I was persuaded to take the role, largely on the grounds that it was just a figurehead role and you had to do virtually nothing. Within a couple of weeks of me taking over there was a national dispute and we were called on to obey a union call to apply sanctions over working conditions. I mention it because it was to influence a future relationship.

The cast of characters working on the *CHAD* was apt to change and there was a significant one about that time when we were joined by Nick. He was tall and quite well built but he had another, more striking, feature. He was the son of the company's owner.

He was working his way round the company in different roles so that, when he inevitably took over as head cod after his Dad, he would know how each department worked and fitted in to the overall aims. He, therefore, had a spell working with the other reporters.

Like Little Chris, he was into cars and seemed to have access to loads of them. I went out with him on one job and he led me to his latest mode of transport. We dropped in at a petrol station on the way to the job and it was like berthing a ship to get this great machine alongside a petrol pump.

The summer came around, as it tends to do, and I was to head back to Sheffield, to the hotel and to Richmond College. Then I heard that Nick would be on the same course. Oh joy!

My reporting role had changed somewhat in that I and another bloke were covering local government, under Harry's leadership. At college, we had newspaper people who came to give us insights into specific aspects like law.

One visit I well remember was from an experienced political correspondent. He was certainly cynical. He told us that local and national politicians as a matter of course played the blame game. When criticised for a lack of action on a problem, the locals said that the national lot did not give them enough money to tackle it. The national lot said they had handed out plenty of money but it had been wasted at local level. That particular political game goes on, and on, and on.

On a visit to Notts County Council's headquarters, I bumped into local politician Michael Cowan. He had something of a reputation. He ran the council budget, as I remember, could be pretty vitriolic in debate and was thought to be on his way up in political circles. He took the trouble to tell me about the need to improve the knowledge of councillors and took me to the members' library, which he was hoping to expand and for it to be better used.

His upward rise came to a halt when he was selected for Labour in the 'safe' seat of Ashfield. The local voters obviously did not take to him because he was defeated, which was something of a sensation for that area. I recall two things in particular about covering that election result. One was that I drove home much quicker than usual after the result. I thought keeping up my speed would sharpen my concentration and cut the risk of me falling asleep.

The other was the press conference the next morning. Mr Cowan was quite accepting and gracious in defeat so it may have been a learning experience that helped shape him for the future.

Labour learned the lesson for the next time the constituency was contested and chose Frank Haynes, who again was a leading figure on the county council. The press joined council members once for a tour of the Queen's Medical Centre as it approached completion. There had been acclaim that this huge complex would be tremendous for the people of Nottinghamshire. Mr Haynes was a voice crying in the wilderness, it seemed, because he predicted that people, especially in the north, would suffer from the trend for putting all medical eggs in one basket. The old 'recovery' hospitals gave a better service, he argued, and not everyone had their own transport to travel to Nottingham for treatment.

There was an incident I enjoyed during a debate at County Hall. A Conservative member who gave the appearance of a retired colonel paused in mid-flow to congratulate Mr Haynes on being selected to fight Ashfield and wishing him well. After the meeting, I walked into the gents to find the chap washing his hands at the sink. I told him that I'd found it refreshing that he should speak up for a political opponent. He replied, "Well, I have different views but I respect the bloke and like him so much I could happily canvass for votes for him." He thought a moment. "Except my fellow Tories would tar and feather me."

Frank Haynes, of course, became the Ashfield MP, which was well deserved but perhaps a bit harsh on the 'sitting tenant'.

Back at college, while it seemed a little strange to be on the same course as Nick, but it was not as bad as I had feared and ended in another life lesson for me.

I was out of the hotel basement this time, with a room

all to myself. My peace was, however, frequently inter-rupted by Nick knocking on my door. He was not exactly highly organised and seemed to arrive at the start of each week without little things like toothpaste.

Late one evening there came a knock at my door, but it was Big Chris rather than Nick. We had each been trying to get our heads round something like the rating system and Chris said she was sick of it and had thumping head-ache. I felt just the same way. We were very comfortable with each other so we turned out the light, lay on the bed and talked about other things.

There was another knock on the door and Nick's head appeared. He switched on the light and then did a double take. He was obviously trying to work out why, if there was anything sexual going on, we were both fully clothed. If there was nothing sexual going on why were we in the dark? The last thing I was going to do was to enlighten him.

We three had a small, hesitant chat before Nick nicked some of my toiletries and went to close the door behind him. I stopped him in his tracks with my call from the bed.

"Oh, Nick."

"Yes?"

"Turn out the light."

He gave us both another bemused look and then did as instructed. I enjoyed that.

Of course, the other reporters knew all about Nick. We were being taught about writing profiles of people and we needed a subject to interview. Nick was taken out to the front of the class and was to answer one question from every member of the class. As my turn approached I felt more and more nervous. I hated that scenario anyway of having to speak in turn; it was nearly as bad as going to a dinner. It came to my turn and I decided that I had to go for it. I asked Nick whether, as the boss' son, he had encountered any antagonism from staff as he had worked his way round each department.

He had already been very honest in his answers to questions like how much was he and Linney's business worth. He looked me straight in the eyes and said he had felt more resentment from reporters than any other department else. I immediately had to acknowledge, to myself at least, that I would have been one of the worst culprits. I still felt the right tactic would have been to send him to the *Derbyshire Times* or similar instead of his own company but that presumably had been someone else's decision. It was another example of getting an uncomfortable glimpse into your own character.

When the course was finished I returned to the reporters' room. Nick, in contrast, returned to an office of his own as another step on his journey to take over running the place.

Staff got a memo saying that in future Mr Linney junior was to be addressed as 'Mr Nicholas.' Fat chance. This was somebody who owned me a dozen tubes of toothpaste.

He had been to see Jeremy and I saw him walking through the reporters' room. I wanted to speak to him anyway and called: "Oi, Nick!" I don't think it quite met the demands of the memo but Nick, to his credit, just grinned and came to talk to me.

What had been a problem, namely going on the same course as the future company chief actually became, I believe, an advantage. We had each come to know each other as individuals.

I was still Father of Chapel or FOC and there were still disputes nationally between union and managements which impinged on local papers like ours. We had a meeting about tactics and what industrial action we would or would not take. I had to go and see Nick to ask whether we would get a projected pay settlement if we interpreted union rulings in such a way to reduce the impact of sanctions on the *CHAD*.

Nick again was honest. He would give no assurance about the money but would be grateful and would try to help us if we helped him. I reported back to the chapel. People were in two minds and so fairly undecided. I was put on the spot and asked whether I thought we could trust Nick to honour not so much his word but the spirit of his message to me. The vote was in his favour and, ultimately, the money was forthcoming. Maybe that was down to straight-talking and toothpaste-scrounging in Sheffield.

There were lighter moments with Nick. I gathered he had a new relationship with a young lady in Nottingham. He also had a new car – a Morgan. I used to be driving into Mansfield and see a little dot in the rear-view mirror of my Morris Minor. In two minutes flat the little dot became a Morgan which paused a foot from my back bumper. Nick would flash his lights, pip and wave and, seconds later, the Morgan would be a little dot ahead. Not that he ever exceeded the speed limit, of course.

One time I parked at the office and noticed that Nick had left on the headlights of his Morgan. His office overlooked the car park and he was looking through his open window. I called up to tell him about the headlights. He threw his car keys down to me and asked me to turn them off. Five minutes later he had tears running down his face from laughing. I got behind the steering wheel and saw an array of levers and knobs like something out of a jet airliner. I turned on fog lights, windscreen wipers, sound system and every other piece of equipment known to car engineer in an effort to turn off the bloody headlights.

I remember that as about the last barmy act of many in my time at the *CHAD*. I had been certified as a qualified journalist. Some unkind individuals said I was already a certified nutcase.

I wanted to see if I, as a plodder, could adapt to the pace of working on a daily newspaper and got my next call to arms at the *Leicester Mercury*.

I finished with a mini-tour including Norfolk and Leicestershire before settling, where else, in Mansfield.

10 A Last Word

SO, WHAT DID I get from my time on the *CHAD*? Certainly memories and 'good experience' and hopefully new skills to offer future employers. And there was one other thing – everything.

When on visits from Norfolk back to Nottinghamshire, I would see Roger on the golf course (where the bounder usually won) and sometimes his wife Frances would treat me to one of her meals. On one such occasion, Roger said he had bumped into Glenys, who was now divorced and living alone, and passed on her phone number to me. I rang it and the rest, as they say, is hysteria.

I later learned that Frances had told Glenys about going to Norfolk to see a friend of Roger's, without Glen realising it was me. I had met Glen's daughter Heather as an angelic little girl. I got to meet her as an adult before I upped and married her mum. Heather and her husband Rob are now a constant source of delight in my life.

Naturally Frances and Roger were among the honoured guests at the wedding of Glenys and Graham and, of course, Roger took the wedding photographs.

Afterword: Pages from the Past

BEING CRICKET FANS, Roger and I were delighted to have the chance to meet Harold Larwood and Bill Voce. Larwood had been one of the central figures in a massive cricketing controversy. Facing a very strong Australian team a plan had been hatched for England to bowl more at the batsmen than the stumps, making the most of Larwood's pace. That Test series then got the tag of Bodyline. All must have been forgiven eventually because Harold emigrated to Australia.

I well remember the occasion of Larwood's return to the area where his cricketing journey began and Roger's iconic picture of the two great pacemen but was surprised when Roger unearthed a background article from the 1970s. I hope it might be of interest.

Larwood Is Back to Bowl Them Over

Two men in their autumn years stroll across a field, chatting, smoking and stirring within each other memories of 40 years ago.

It is a common enough sight anywhere, but the memories of these men are shared by people all over the world, and their names – Harold Larwood and Bill Voce – still cause a stir all these years after their exploits on the cricket field placed them at the centre of an international row.

And as they stroll across a Nuncargate field it is as if the intervening years had never been. For this was the way they used to travel home after playing for Notts and helping to create a glorious chapter in the club's history.

They would take the same path which cuts behind the Cricketers' Arms and usually exchange a few words with the miners leaning over the wall at the back of the pub. They were always eager to learn the latest score and how Harold had made the batsmen blanch.

Bill Voce (left) and Harold Larwood, former England pace bowlers, revisit Nuncargate where they began their cricketing careers.

This scene was re-enacted recently when Harold Larwood officially opened Nuncar Court old people's complex. He was on a sponsored trip from Australia, where he now lives, and the event proved to be a real homecoming.

It was a scene straight from the pages of a story book as the local hero met again friends who watched him develop into the most feared pace bowler of the generation and followed his career as he sent cricket stumps flying on grounds all around the world.

For example Sam Reeves, now 91, who was also born in Nuncargate, was a close friend of Bob Larwood and can remember his son Harold being born at their home at 17 Chapel Street.

Sam would call in to see Bob Larwood most days and when he started a family of his own Bob gave him the same crib to use in which his own children had slept. Times were hard for most in the tiny mining community and a crib was something of a prized possession.

When Harold, now in his seventies, returned to the scene of his childhood memories it was fitting that he should be asked to open Nuncar Court for the buildings were constructed on the recreation ground where he first paced out his run-up and developed the bowling action that was to become so famous.

Another childhood friend, Jack Handley, is now 70, and lives at Albion Street, Mansfield. He remembered Harold as a happy-go-lucky character at Kirkby Wodhouse school but when he started bowling for Nuncargate, even at the age of 14, his blinding pace left most batsmen anything but happy.

Nuncargate was an area rich in cricketing talent as the legend about shouting down Annesley pit shaft for an England fast bowler shows. Another local resident remembers that the village used to be known as Newkin, and he can remember Larwood playing with the local lads on the recreation ground.

"Quite often a bronzed man with a pork pie trilby hat would saunter down from his home in Fisher Street towards the Cricketers' Arms for his daily pint and pause for a while to watch the lads at play. And that man, too, bore a name that will remain forever in the annals of the cricketing world – Joe Hardstaff senior."

He recalled how he would walk with Joe Hardstaff junior. "And he would persist in balancing himself precariously upon the pavement edge taking a hefty swipe here and there at an imaginary ball with an imaginary bat. Even at that tender age Joe was determined to follow in his father's footsteps." That determination resulted in 1,636 in his 23 tests for England. In those days test matches were not so limited in time and one of Harstaff junior's greatest innings was an undefeated 169 out of an England total of 903 for seven declared in 1938. Geoff Boycott would have been in his element.

And a little further up the hill from the recreation ground lived another youthful cricketer, Bill Voce, whose destiny was to be linked with that of Larwood.

Bill Voce remembers walking down to the recreation ground to train on a wicket that was full of chock holes where children could play marbles. Not even the bowler knew where the ball would go once it pitched. "I think it was good training though," he said.

There were few houses on the Kirkby side of the road, except for a farm in those days.

The local cricket pitch was on a field behind the Cricketers' and when teenaged Larwood began to play for Nuncar his opponents, like so many people since, must have been struck by his lack of size –unlike the popular image of the broad-shouldered, broad-beamed pace bowler.

Harold, like his father, became a miner and he said

that it helped to build up his back muscles and so his fear-some pace.

He moved on to play for Annesley Colliery, Mansfield Colliery, Notts, and then to make his test debut against Australia in 1926. He took the first of his 78 test wickets when Sutcliff caught Charlie Macartney for 39 and went on to play in the fifth test as a 21-year-old when England clinched the Ashes.

His bowling exploits were to make him world famous but Larwood was no mug with a bat either. In the first test of the 1928-29 series against Australia he made 70 and, with Patsy Hendren, put on a record 124 for the eighth wicket. It was one of his best matches as he also collected his best test figures of six for 32.

His left arm opening partner Bill Voce had to wait longer before making his test debut in 1929 but he went on to take 98 wickets in 27 tests.

As they enjoyed a drink with their wives recently, Larwood cast an interesting light on the times. He was able to date a famous picture of himself taken at the point of delivery because of the sash round his waist. They were later replaced by supports in the top of the trousers.

It was on the tour of Australia in 1932-33 that Larwood and Voce found themselves in the centre of a row which became a national as well as a sporting issue.

Legend had it that the theory of bodyline bowling was worked out on the boat 'down under.' The bowlers let fly with short-pitched deliveries while a cluster of short legs waited for the snick as the batsman took defensive action and two men were posted deep for the mistimed hook.

England won the first test by 10 wickets with Larwood taking 5 for 96 and 5 for 28 and Voce collecting 4 for 110. Australia squared the series before hostilities really erupted in the third test.

Woodfull was hit a sickening blow over the heart by a ball from Larwood and he was later quoted as saying that only one side was playing crcket. Protests were sent to the MCC but they replied that unless the laws were changed there was nothing to prevent that type of bowling being used. The Australians replied that the bowling was dangerous to players.

The Australian crowds – always enthusiastic – were not too interested in the finer points of the laws of the game, and mounted police had to stand by to prevent a riot.

The controversy was discussed in the Press, in bars and on street corners throughout the cricketing world and became the subject of music hall jokes. Whether it was "cricket" was debatable but it was certainly effective as the tourists won the last three tests.

A cartoon in the *Australian Cricketer* showed that there was humour behind the white heat of events on the cricket field. It depicted a coffin labelled 'Bodyline esq' with Larwood and England captain Jardine following behind, wearing black armbands and weeping profusely.

In the fifth test Larwood again demonstrated that he was no mean batsman. He was sent in as night watchman and was finally caught at mid-on two short of his century.

It must have been a relief for Larwood to return home but any personal antagonism towards him died away. When he and his wife, Lois, emigrated to Australia they were given quite a welcome by the Australian people.

And when they return to their home next week they can look forward to celebrating their golden wedding. They have five daughters and 13 grandchildren.

The years have rolled by but in sport controversy tends to follow controversy. Bill Voce, who now lives in Hucknall, shares with many others the concern about the effect on test cricket of Kerry Packer's cricket circus. He pointed out that county clubs rely on proceeds from tests to survive and all levels of cricket will be effected.

Harold Larwood, too, has some interesting reflections on the modern game. He thought, for instance, that pace bowlers today have a far easier time than their predecessors who had to bowl all day on occasions. In the opening test of that famous – or infamous – series he bowled in the second innings with his strained side strapped up.

He maintains too that he would always bowl flat out.

It certainly must have been hard work, either working at the pit or later hurling down a cricket ball throughout the day, often not getting home until 9pm.

Harold Larwood and his wife Lois stand outside 17 Chapel Street, Nuncargate, where he was born.

His wife, Lois, was also a local girl so it was to be expected that the couple should receive a real welcome when they returned to Kirkby. Mrs Larwood had not seen her sister, Mrs Irene Burton, for about nine years so there were some tears to be shed.

But the cricketing legend seemed surprised by the welcome he received from the local people which turned the event from an official function to a real homecoming.

Children crowded round him for autographs, groups of spectators waited for him to appear and old campaigners discussed his early days and his exploits on the other side of the world.

Bill Voce, his opening partner, quietly took a back seat while Harold chatted to locals and caught up on years of gossip.

Then the two pace partners were able to share a few quiet moments of cricketing memories.

It may prove to be Larwood's last visit to Britain and his feats may be surpassed but one thing remains certain.

Harold Larwood has a place in the hearts of the Nuncargate people who grew up with him, and a place in the imaginations of generations of cricket fans still to come.

Brass and the boys bid a fond farewell.